Beyond the Garden

by

James B. Clay

authorHOUSE™

1663 LIBERTY DRIVE, SUITE 200
BLOOMINGTON, INDIANA 47403
(800) 839-8640
WWW.AUTHORHOUSE.COM

First published by AuthorHouse 09/22/04

ISBN: 1-4184-8477-6 (sc)

Printed in the United States of America
Bloomington, Indiana

This book is printed on acid-free paper.

TABLE OF CONTENTS

Isle of Paradise

Poets write their lyrics, some in song,
About this isle, to which we belong,
Of tragedy, humor, drama, love,
Human life, give and take, push and shove;
All players on shifting sand, a stage,
Where the storms do both abate and rage.

We know death, looked at her in the face,
Taking a life we can n'er replace!
We also know of our offsprings' plight,
Their struggle to keep wisdom in sight,
And their search for a place in the sun,
Temptations, the gamut they will run.

Still as bitter-sweet doth grow the night,
With daily stress, an ongoing fight,
There's a haven with meaningful rest,
Not out there, to aid you in your quest,
An isle of bliss, a port in the storm,
On this earth, a Son to keep you warm.

Thus the clouds fade and give way to day,
Yet, those pains and hurts still have their sway,
For you are not exempt from such things,
But the courage to face them, he brings;
Fate, unlike a fickle toss of dice,
He creates into paradise.

Lovingly dedicated by Jim and B J Clay to Kevin Hunter, Randal Scott, Craig Lee, John Kevin and Fred, as well as Freddie Clay's children, Tanna, Stacy, and Jarine. Not that we have arrived, and most certainly not when you were babies, we were only fellow passengers searching for truth. We ask for your forgiveness for every time we let you down or disappointed you, but when we were a child, we spoke as a child; when we were full grown we tried to put away childish things, seeking for our place, emitting different sounds (December, 2003).

Preface

There were two major influences in my life as a child that helped me to see beyond the garden. As a child, my brother Freddie would beg me to tell him a story. Well I told him all of the regular stories that I knew, like, <u>The Three Bears,</u> <u>The Three Little Pigs</u> and <u>Little Red Riding Hood,</u> et al. Now and then, I made up a story to tell him starting with these and other stories as a basis for my departure. Of course, I used a great deal of embellishment. At night when we were in bed, he would say, "Tell me a story." I began with the usual; but he said, "No, tell me one of yours, I like them better." And off into the adventure we went.

The stories herein related as if we were in the feather bed at night are grown up stories not told in that pristine setting; however, they do reflect some of the ideas we had about God, the Bible and life. Non-biblical stories are intended as a vehicle to jump start the reader into some of the truths found in those gems of wisdom from contemporaries of people who wrote the Scriptures. Hopefully they will help us to find our destiny. Someone may indeed ask why include the other creation stories? They represent the great diffusion of ideas discovered in the land of our beginning. They also have a preponderance of evidence about the similarities of thought patterns of ancient man, our brother. In whatever form truth finds itself, regardless of its origination, it contains heavenly nuggets.

Please don't get lost in the imagery of the stories. It will be easy for the reader to believe the story of the Garden of Eden, for we grew up with the narrative. However, unless we come to realize it is a story which relates a gem, not a historical fact, then we have to answer some important questions. Like: 1. How did God who is Spirit walk in the garden? 2. How did he talk to the first couple? 3. How did Adam go to sleep and not know he was having an operation? Did God just reach inside of Adam to pull out a rib? When Adam awakes, he jumps up in glee because he has a full grown wo-wo-woman for a playmate? What, no recovery time? And don't try to tell me he didn't know Eve was naked. 4. The big question everyone wants to know is, of course, where did Cain get a woman to marry? His sister? Okay, I'll give you that. But why is she punished along with Cain to go where he goes in shame? Was it just because she is a lowly woman? There are many jewels in this crown. To absorb the message within the trimmings will free the adherent from any such questions.

I did not know it at the time, but I would discover in years to come, all the Bible stories I grew up hearing had been fashioned in the thought pattern of their day. Their knowledge was limited to the day in which they lived, yet not exempt from other beliefs and laws. In other words, their religion was not a hot house variety. Some of the stories were told to relate a truth and they (the story teller) would add bits of lore from the surrounding countries and their gods.

The Hebrew was one people, the Greeks another, who cared for tradition, each wanting to try to put their story into a historical context. The Israelites wrote their history with the only tools they had. They used vellum, stone and papyrus leaves to record their history. For a long period of time it was handed down by the art of telling stories. No matter how precise they told them however, they lost something in the translation. Take the phrase from the movie "Casablanca", which has been interpreted, "Play it again Sam." The actual saying went something like this, "Play it; you played it for her; now play it for me!" After writing began, bits of the stories were written down by an unknown writer, some think perhaps Moses. As the years progressed, fragments of these appeared, broader in scope, by sources known as J, P, E, D and H edited by priests who began to place them into logical order around 444 B.C. (For an excellent discourse on this, read, "The Ten Commandments," by A. Powell Davies). Mixed in with their history was the myth of the hero or God to make the scene an important one. In fact, the purpose of myth was to illumine the mind to those who will be hearing the story with unmistakable imagery about some religious experience or historical event. Case in point, when angels appeared to men, they were never meant to be real; it was a way to emphasize spiritual insight. In Genesis 18:1ff, three men came to visit Abraham. One Abraham recognized as the Lord. Apparently the other two were his angels. Right away a meal was prepared for them to eat. The writer never intended for the reader to believe God and angels literally visited or ate a meal, but they did want to show how important the spiritual insight was and, ergo, they stressed the image to make the encounter emphatic.

They were messengers sent to open the minds of Abraham and Sarah, his wife.

In the next chapter, two angels appeared in Sodom to visit with Lot. They were agents sent to tell Lot and his family to leave. The reason was simply, because of the wickedness there, the Lord would destroy Sodom. A strange thing happened while they visited Lot. The men of the city came to Lot to demand that he give the men to them so they might abuse them sexually. The common theme of most sermons preached on this text indicates that the sexual acts were the reason for the destruction. However, one of the more prominent teachings of the era in which they live, in almost every culture of that time, inferred that strangers were welcomed with open arms and the same treated with great respect.

One only has to read the "Odyssey" by Homer to follow Odysseus in his journeys to see the kinds of receptions strangers were afforded. Hence because of their abuse of the stranger and with no regard for the sanctity of life, no compassion, the people of Sodom lose their chance for life, liberty and the pursuit of happiness.

Therefore, the purpose of the narrative was to explain the reason for their coming. A significant event in time was made more relevant with the arrival of God's messengers, or angels as stated. They sat in darkness. They saw a great light. Their eyes opened to truth. Unfortunately many have felt all their lives that the Bible required them to believe every word as written. I saw a lady with a slogan on her t-shirt which read, "God said it, I believe it; that settles it." If it said angels, it meant angels. Apparently when she read the Bible, metaphors changed into reality.

Let it be said, however, that Biblical stories have for centuries consoled countless millions to put Christ as the center of their universe. They say he is of crucial importance for all. When religious myths thus work effectively, it is as absurd to criticize them for being religious myths not supported by scientific fact. Just as ridiculous, it would be unjust for one to insist they are scientific fact and proceed to draw historical and scientific conclusions from them.

The second event that had a remarkable effect on me was the times I would meditate under a large pine tree in our front yard. I had a little red wagon that I pulled everywhere I went. Upon arrival at my destination, my tree of consolation, I sat in the wagon to contemplate. The most frequent thoughts concerned the origin of God. I had been told that in the beginning there was no one but him; and, out of nothing, he created the world and all that was in it. Now this blew my mind. I lounged in my wagon for hours to try to imagine nothing but a live person hovering around for eternity. Then one day he spoke and the world came into being. . . Perhaps this one thing led to my quest to find some answers more than any other. From where did God come? I asked my parents where I came from and I was given a long tale about a stork. In the ole outhouse where the older boys had found their phalluses, I found out the truth. I really wanted to believe the former story.

To get beyond the garden has been a life time dream. A more profound inspiration seems to compel me back to the garden. Herein the quest begins. Not that I have arrived, but I have found some answers which bring a great deal of satisfaction. The odd part about it, I have come to them on my own only to find later others who feel the same way I do. What a joy to know others are searching also. The search requires us to go to the beginning of time according to all of the knowledge handed down. Each has its own way of trying to express truth of an endeavor to find meaning, or freedom to be human, in the midst of struggles which surround every person. Hopefully the readers will put their own experiences into the mix to find their own meaning for existence. Remember, from where we come has a lot to do with where we are going, but it should not pigeon-hole us either. Also, I hope the readers have a private church where they can discuss these issues over against the prevailing thought patterns of our day. As for me, I am only a seeker on a quest to know myself. The hard part is to put off all those things which I have held for so long which bring me down.

I knew not the terms used to describe thoughts of which I had discovered prior to my inquiries. Writers like Rudolph Bultmann, Erich Fromm, Will Campbell, Joseph Campbell, Scott Peck, and Nathaniel Hawthorne, to name a few, guided me to a better understanding of the theology I came to hold. Terms like transcendence, antinomianism, theism, deism, and monotheism became subjects of pursuit. Not only were these authors helpful, technology gave me the internet where any subject desired rested at my fingertips.

The storyline falls in three sections. Section one attempts to show that all systems of thought about the creation of mankind infer that all came from the earth by the creative force of life which unmistakably shows us as brothers and sisters. Section two involves the nature by which all men and women experience the Garden of Eden. The womb is the first place; while the magical world of childhood follows with both showing certain imprints which shape our lives. Section three then endeavors to show how those events shape our lives with an idea of how to come to our true selves by transcending (even thought we may keep some of our earlier beliefs) to a realm of worth and value exhorted by Jesus Christ and other leaders of world religions.

I am grateful for my wife B.J.Clay who had the will to listen, to inspire. Also, she and I would discuss for hours concepts and ideas contained here. She would do proof reading to offer suggestions as to how to make this easier to understand. Most importantly, she taught me how to use the d... computer. In addition, my friend Maurice Turner took time to hear me out. He may not have agreed, but he wanted me to put this in writing. His encouragement urged me to proceed.

THE BROTHERHOOD OF MAN

The Garden

"Ok boys, it is time for bed," Momma would say; so Freddie and I would go to our bedroom in the back which had been transformed from the old kitchen. An ell had been added to make a new kitchen and we had us a room to ourselves. Just as we snuggled in the bed, he spoke, "Will you tell me a story?" Whether I wanted too was not an option, so I began.

"In the beginning, about a million or so years ago, there was nothing. Where we lay now there was nothing but water and there was darkness everywhere. Remember, darkness abounded. Now there was only one person living and his name was Lord or God, depending on which version of the act of creation you read. The Spirit of God, as we shall call him, moved over the deep; he decided to put some sky which he called Heaven. Next he caused to come into being the land masses and separated the water from the land which he called earth. Then he caused the earth to produce vegetation; next the sun and the moon came into being; then birds and fish and animals from the sea including huge leviathans appeared. Animals that would live on the land came next into existence at his command; on the sixth day he created from the dust of the earth you and me. Well, not you and me, but our kind. He said to the animals; 'Let us make man in my own image, fashioned like you, but with a spirit of me endowed.' And it came to pass. On the seventh day, he rested from his labor. All this had been rather laborious for him, so he deserved a break."

"You mean he did all that in six days," Freddie asked incredulously?

"So the old folks tell us, but between you and me, it took many thousands of years before the first man ever came to be on this earth," said I. "But we will get to that later; right now we need to stay with our story."

"First, tell me where God came from," he asked innocently?

"He just was and that is all I know," I answered in the best way I knew how.

"I find that hard to believe," said he. And so did I!

After a long pause, "We will try to answer that one as we move along," I finally replied. "As for now, the Hebrew had a very orderly mind and the number of days corresponded to the days of the week. Logically, the writer put things in a numerical sequence to say out of the chaos God brought perfection. The writer never meant to say this all happened in six days. He was writing in a day where other creation stories abounded; he wanted to tell the story of creation according to his historical understanding. The only way he knew was an orderly account. Besides the number seven represented a symbol of perfection to the Jews of his day (Dr. Ray Robbins treats this subject in "The Revelation of Jesus Christ"). Now don't you tell Momma this, because she will want to know where you got this ridiculous story about creation not being fashioned in six days!

Let's move on. On the earth that God made, he placed a garden and in it he put the first couple, Adam and Eve. He told them to have children and control the earth with all its glory. The world as the writer knew it was like a three story building, heaven, hell and earth. Today scientists have proven that we are a vast universe, with others like ourselves even beyond.

The second rendition of the creation of Adam and Eve took on a different slant. It seemed God created Adam and he was not a happy camper because he had no other human to converse with him. God saw his displeasure; and wanting to please, he realized Adam needed a helpmate. When Adam went to bed, God took from his side a rib and made woman, Eve. When Adam awoke there she was. He was well pleased; and, he let her and God know by saying something like: 'bones of my bones; flesh of my flesh; she shall be called woman because she was taken out of man.'"

Freddie interrupted, "Won't this make women unhappy to know that they came from man and not men from them? Say that is heavy stuff. Besides it might lead man to think he is superior to woman, don't you think so too brother?"

"Nah this can never happen, because I am sure the writer meant to say that the woman was made out of the same stuff as the man;" yet the writer was from a patriarchal society and I wondered in the silence that followed for the next few minutes if the writers were putting the woman in her place according to the view of the world from a dominating male perspective? Did not Paul in his letters so imply?

"To continue, God instructed the pair to tend the garden and to eat of every tree there but two. God placed these trees in the garden as a symbol of 'Thou shalt not'. One tree held the knowledge of good and evil and the other bestowed the ability to be immortal, as a God. 'The one forbidden thing', as it has been proclaimed, required them not to touch or to eat else they would die. Of course it opened up a whole new approach, for when we are told we can't do something, it only increases our curiosity.

Take the story of "Bluebeard" for example. Bluebeard is a very rich man. He marries a local girl and he gives to her all of his possessions to use as well as money to spend. However, he says to her, 'Don't go in to the little room off the parlor. If you do I will have to cause you great fear.' Well, he just goofs when he tells her not to do that. Curiosity gets the best of her. She finally takes the key; she opens the door and she goes into the room. She is taken by horror. On the floor is a lot of old blood, and lined along the wall, stand the bodies of all his ex-wives" (For the full story, go to: MSN.com; then, "Bluebeard").

"What kind of trees grow like those two in the garden," he asked suddenly?

"I don't know, but Momma says her preacher calls them apple trees and he should know, trained in the Bible and all. I can say this though, it wasn't the apple in the tree that caused Adam and Eve to sin; it was the pair on the ground!" We laughed.

"Let me hear some more," he uttered.

"Where are we, oh yes, like Bluebeard's wife, one day Eve goes to the tree to look. In the garden lives a creature which is called a serpent. He is the sexiest thing in the garden and he speaks to Eve."

"Now wait a minute," Freddie proclaimed! "I know snakes can't talk."

"Well this one did, the Bible says it plain. Most people believe it was the fallen angel Lucifer, from John Bunyan's book 'Paradise Lost'. But you know how Hollywood does, with special effects and all," I ad-libbed! "Anyway, he speaks to her to persuade her to partake. After a little banter and they verbally fence some, she tries one and it is good. So she calls Adam to tell him how good it is and he gulps it down. Well, they see themselves naked as a jay bird. Boy the face of each turns beet red. I bet they were saying, 'The sand has hit the fan now.' They hide in the garden. No use, though. The jig is up. The shepherd of the garden comes looking for them, knowing they did badly. Well, they decide to come out of hiding to confess. 'What have you done,' he asked Adam? Adam replies, 'Eve ate of the fruit of the forbidden tree; she gave to me and I did eat.' He looks to Eve, and she replies, 'The snake, it was the serpent who told me to eat.' No need to look at the reptile, he didn't have a leg to stand on." Freddie guffawed.

"Boys, you better hush up in there, tomorrow is a school day!"

"Go on," he whispered. "But talk softly."

"Let's see, okay, God punishes them right there. He tells Adam he will have to work hard the rest of his life tilling the soil to make a living. Eve will have to bear children in pain. He really comes down hard on the snake and Eve. As far as the serpent, he is cursed for the rest of his life. You know that is true because very few people like snakes. If a turtle, dog, cat or an animal from the forest crosses the road, we go out of our way to miss them. Not a snake, we swerve all over the road to kill it. And there are some good snakes. But some folks think a snake is a snake and they don't care whether it is good or bad.

Because of their failure to obey, the whole human race and Mother Earth herself fall. Paul calls this original sin. We are born in sin and have to die in sin. All the bad, evil things that mankind does stem from the first couple's failure. Not only man, but all the so called 'acts of God' come from this moment. Evil comes into the world through the sins of Adam and Eve (For an excellent discourse on the origin of evil, read John Hick, ("Evil and the God of Love"). Some say this happened so that a greater good could come in the person of Jesus, who would come to redeem us from inherited evil. It seems God predestined this.

Anyway, God booted them out of the playing field; the way to the land of tranquility lay ahead. He made sure they could not return by placing some lion-bird people, cherubs, at the gate; he then put a flaming, twisting sword to make sure they didn't return to eat of the tree of life."

"Wow, don't you think God was mean to all of us, just because Adam failed," Freddie asked, rather put out by the turn of events? "How can the free will of man and preordination coexist," he mumbled, not really expecting an answer?

Quite frankly, I wondered where he came up with this. "We will get to this another time, as for now it is time we went to sleep." In a few moments, he was fast asleep, and I lay for awhile pondering all these things in my heart.

> Then there was heard, a most celestial sound,
> Soft, sweet music coming from the feathered down,
> As peaceful sleep brought colorful dreams,
> From a story seemingly without seams;
> When the Titans with swords on him bore,
> They were only astonished at his lore,
> And the raging winds forgot to roar.

Babylonian View of Creation

No one knew how many steps we made the next day, in and out of play. Nor did we, but no matter how tired we grew, the inevitable question came, "Can you tell me another story brother?"

"I suppose so," I answered, "What would you like to hear?"

"You told me about other creation stories, so please let me hear about them."

"Then we shall begin there," I replied. "In the beginning of time water was over the face of the earth, for land had not yet been formed. There existed Apsu, the father, Tiamat, the mother, and Mummu, the son ("Documents from Old Testament Times", edited by D. Winton Thomas). Now no other gods existed, for they had not yet been born. Tiamat gave birth to children over the years and their children sired other gods. One of the grandchildren was named Anu; he in turn would clone a son in the likeness of himself, the mighty Ea. All seemed well in the holy water, until the grandchildren started to get on Apsu's nerves. He summoned his favorite child, the older son Mummu, and asked for his counsel. Mummu told him they should take it to the queen, Tiamat, which they did. She, upon hearing their report, simply replied, 'Children will be children,' in her most patient, loving way.

Until this time, the water in which they lived was the same. However, evil stirred the caldron as the loving, obedient son, Mummu, accepted not the counsel of the mother. 'Father, one whom I adore; we cannot let this counsel rest. Why not slay all the Queen's lovers; then you shall find peace?' This pleased the old man and he took Mummu upon his knee; as he sat upon the lap of his beloved father, he hugged and kissed him with glee (The elder brother perhaps?).

Somehow Ea got wind of the strategy. He proceeded to entice the pair to his home; there he used a magic spell to put them to sleep. Ea removed the royal dress from his venerable grandfather; he then murdered him. As for the shifty older brother, he grabbed him by the nose and he tied him with a rope to lead him around the universe in shame. Of course, Ea proclaimed himself king. He built a mansion fit for a king; he married Damkina; and they had a son, Marduk. Marduk, the future king of the earth, made a gigantic impression on the parents, their creation . . . Therefore Ea conferred upon Marduk twice the strength of himself along with special spiritual insight.

The story of Ea represents in the finest fashion the story of Oedipus." (This story comes from a delightful little book entitled, "Classic Myths in English Literature," edited by C.M. Gayley).

"Who's Oedipus," Freddie interrupted?

"Legend tells us he was a son of a suspicious king. The king, warned in a dream to get rid of the boy, complies. He gives him to a shepherd with instructions to kill him. However, the sheep tender feels sorry for Oedipus; he thus spares his life. One day, Oedipus returns to his father's kingdom when he himself received an oracle that he would become instrumental in the death of his father. Not wanting this to come true, he begins his journey. Upon his arrival, he meets his father and his chariot driver. Since both Oedipus and the king are in chariots, one has to get off the one-lane road. Neither driver cares to budge. You know the king will have none of this, so he instructs the driver to slay one of Oedipus' horses, which he does. An infuriated Oedipus, as a consequence of the driver's action, in turn, murders the both of them on the spot, not knowing the king was indeed his father. He thus continues on his journey to the city of Thebes, the realm of his father, the king.

When he gets there, the city is in turmoil because the people have been terrorized by a huge monster named Sphinx. It seems Sphinx stops all passengers on the road to the city to ask them a riddle. Those that answer it correctly may pass; those who do not die. 'None so far has succeeded,' they explain to Oedipus. Undaunted he goes to see the monster. 'The riddle is this,' says Sphinx. 'What has four legs in the morning, two legs in the noon, and three at night?' 'Man,' answers Oedipus, 'because before he can walk he has to crawl on all fours. In the prime of his life, he walks on two legs. When he is old, he walks with a cane.' The monster becomes so mortified that he jumps off a cliff to kill himself. Well, needless to say, the people of Thebes are so happy that they make him king and guess what?"

"What," Freddie asks breathlessly?

"They give him the queen, his mother to marry?" Only he doesn't find out until later he has killed his father and then he has married his mother."

Then Freddie asks," Do you think we have an Oedipus complex brother?"

"No," I replied, only I did not know that he for the next few years of his life would suffer from it, as well as I for the next fifty some odd years.

"Please go on with your story," he states after a minute or two of contemplation.

"Let me think, where I was….oh yes, Ea and his wife have given birth to Marduk. After his birth an embassy of rebel gods, led by the Queen's son, Kingu, approach Tiamat; they convince her to avenge the death of her husband. We now see a very different woman than the one we met earlier. She girds her loins for battle; she becomes a woman scorned. When the dynamic duo of Ea and Anu learn of her plans for war, fear envelops their souls. Ea consults his grandfather who instructs him to fight along with Anu, his dad. One is to use magic and the other is to use authority. Neither works; so they approach Marduk to fight her with his power. He agrees provided he will be pronounced king. Willing to try anything to save their lives, they agree. Marduk proceeds to do battle. Eventually he succeeds; in victory he takes her body, divides it into two pieces, taking the upper to create the astronomical seasons, including the sun and the moon. Next he takes the lower half to create the land mass called earth."

"It looks like to me that now we have Mother Earth created out of woman. Is this why we call earth Mother, because life came from her," He inquired?

"If you recall from the Bible story, one version of creation says that God took dust from the earth to fashion man, hence I would have to say yes," I replied.

"Yes, but you haven't mentioned the birth of man yet. How did that happen," he wanted to know?

I began, "You will recall that Marduk said if he fights his grandmother, he would become king." "Uhhuh." "Well, right away he takes charge. He requires the gods to start to build him a palace, none ever before its equal. All they do is complain because they have to toil; so they call a tête-à-tête to decide a course of action. In the ensuing council, the gods decide to create man to do the work. Marduk decides to punish Kingu, the god responsible for stirring up Tiamat. They bring Kingu into the hall; they kill him; from his blood, they create man to do the work on behalf of the gods.

You can say that since Kingu was her son that the birth of man came from Mother Earth. Also, both stories refer to the deep, God brooding over the deep in the first and here they dwell in the deep. One other point of interest remains. Both follow a common sequence for the act of creation. Of course, I don't have to point out the obvious differences." I looked to see if he had heard, but he had dropped off to sleep:

In the peaceful sleep of sweet repose,
One may dance on balletic toes,
With visions of the garden gate,
While on the morrow, resume that oedipal gait!

Greek Mystery Tradition

"Brother," he opined, "Why is it people can always look at non-biblical myths to see the illogical nature of them, but when reading their own lore, they can't see the trees for the forest?"

"I don't know the answer to that one Freddie; but again, we only look at these myths to see if we find a tiny bit of a clue from whence we came, some kernel of truth on which we can hang our hats, so to speak. Hopefully we can learn that if the story contains a myth, even in the Bible, there is more to it than meets the eye. If we are to dig out the message and meaning of the author, it will require great insight; like the insight the authors of the New Testament realized Jesus had, who after his death, credited his vision to a virgin birth," I added parenthetically. "Because the story comes in a mystery, we don't have to throw out the baby with the bath water; it represents the author's intent and purpose which houses the truth." He giggled. I went further, "Neither do we have to believe the myth to accept the pearl of wisdom."

"I believe that," he stated emphatically.

After a time of reflection, "What is our story for tonight," he inquired?

"How about the Greek mystery rendition of creation," I stated, not really asking a question. One of the stories contains information from the legacy of Dionysus, the god of bread and wine (see Gayley). He has many names, but one of the more picturesque ones entitles him Bacchus (For a view of Bacchus go to MSN.com; enter Bacchus). Bacchus, as you will recall, has a parade in his honor at the Mardi Gras festival in New Orleans each year. He represents the Greek god of wine and cheer. Many wine miracles have been performed at festivals in his honor through the years. According to the legend, Bacchus dies each year in the winter solstice, and he returns in the spring to life, especially in the grape harvest. To his adherents, he embodies the promise of the resurrection of the dead. As one drinks of the wine and eats of the bread, they commemorate their own salvation."

"Hey," Freddie exclaimed, "that sounds like our church on Saturday where we celebrate the Eucharist!"

"Exactly," I retorted. "Anyway, Dionysus' mother is Persephone, daughter of Demeter, Queen of the earth, and mother of all vegetation. Demeter leaves Persephone in a cave, guarded by the two serpents that pull her chariot. Demeter decides she should tell Zeus, the father of Persephone, where she resides. So Zeus goes to her disguised as a serpent, copulates, and Dionysus comes into being. Now the wife of Zeus hears of this. Needless to say, she does not like the turn of events; so she sends some Titans, creatures which come from volcanic eruptions of the earth, created to cause corruption in the world, to kill the child. They capture him; they maim him and then the creatures feast on his body. When Zeus learns of the event, he enters the cave; he kills the Titans and he creates man from their ashes. Hence man now has two parts of creation like in the Bible story; from the dust, man comes forth, with the spirit of God in him. In a similar manner, the Titans give mortality to man; Dionysus, digested by the Titans, issues immortality to mankind."

"Dust to dust, ashes to ashes," Freddie croons. "Tell me how Bacchus comes back to life?"

"Well," said I, "one of the goddesses, Athena, saves his heart from the Titans to give to Zeus. He takes it to put in his thigh through a slit he makes to vouchsafe the baby until Bacchus can be reborn."

"Boy that sounds a lot like the birth narrative of Jesus. Only there the angel Gabriel, or a dove, comes to tell her she will have a baby. The angel says the Holy Spirit will descend upon her to impregnate her through the ear, so to speak," he prophesied, matter of factually, without expecting an answer, as he did quite often! "Jesus born of the earth, Mary, mortal, and conceived by the Spirit, immortal. He too came into being just as Adam and Eve did. Only Jesus would have the ability to see through the darkness of those blinded by tradition. Like Isaiah 9:2 (KJV):

> "The people that walked in darkness have seen a great
> light:
> They that dwell in the land of the shadow…upon them
> hath the light shined."

Our first ancestors had to grope from day to day to answer questions about their origin. Thus they had to create their idea of God; they had to come to grips with their quest to find him as well as to put their understanding in fresh, new words. In other words, the first humans in an existential environment fashioned their myths around their concept of God."

"Yeah," I answered, "and you will remember that Adam called his wife Eve, which means mother of all living things. Jesus' birth is a spiritual one, which I will explain later. For now, suffice it to say, he was born of Mary, fully human, with the same capacity of development as you and I. In fact, the story of Jesus parallels the story of the birth of Adam. From nothing but the earth, God creates man. From Mary, woman of the earth, God creates Jesus. Throughout his life, he will demonstrate the purpose of God for you and me. Everything that happens in his life occurs in the physical realm. 'Much to do about nothing' happens when modern man places the ecstatic experience over against the humanity of Jesus. Whatever the euphoric feeling contains, it has to reconcile with Jesus' earthly life and teachings. The experience must lead to a deeper commitment to a discovery of our own humanity."

"I can see how we get caught up in the spiritual, heavenly aspect;" he interrupted, "enamored with the spiritual side of life we forget the bodily aspect; they go hand in hand, flesh and spirit, body and soul. If we play the spirit against the body, we will put the main emphasis in heaven only to lose the transcendence of the whole person here on earth. So, the spirituality of Jesus leads us back to the garden where we find true peace on earth! If we choose to ignore the Godly aspect of our creation, we will live out our lives incomplete, void of meaning and hope."

I answered his observation, "Looking back over Jesus' life, the disciples saw him (their eyes opened) as the son of God. During his time on earth as a human, none understood him. Throughout his life they kept trying to remake him into their image of the Messiah. He steadfastly refused. In fact his favorite designation for himself was Son of Man. (See my project, The Humanity of Jesus. . .). He fused into the title the suffering and shame of the cross, which only until after his death did his followers see. Thus the legend arose in Matthew (1:20) that Jesus was begotten by the Holy Spirit or by the power of the most high (Luke 1:35)." It could be argued that Luke never said it was a virgin birth, but that he said God would be active in the event as well as throughout his life. At any rate, the idea of the virgin birth of Jesus came after his death, not before. Each person has the same capabilities as Jesus; however we don't have the desire or the character to seek to find our true destiny. We devise a set of rules which represent holiness and we are content with our own idea of God. Hopefully we can see later what I mean by 'God reduced to our own image.'"

About that time the voice of tradition boomed, "You boys better cut out that foolishness and get to sleep!" I didn't know at the time how many times I would hear the first part of that sentence in my life, but I would.

> Truth distilled in tradition,
> Carves a strange rendition,
> A soul with a swagger,
> Yet carries a two edged dagger;
> While truth unshackled from its bounds,
> Renders a song with fresh, intoned sounds.

A View with a Twist

The feather bed with its coziness and security was not the only source of solace for Freddie and me. Out behind the house in which we lived, there stood an old log barn. It had two partitions, divided in the middle by a passageway large enough to allow two wagons to pass at the same time. The right side contained a room with a door to lock to safely store the feed for the livestock. On the left, the hay compartment, huge in its capacity, arose. Behind and in front of the two compartments, Papa had built the stalls to feed the animals with babies and to contain the cows when he milked. The barn represented freedom, privacy and warmth. On a certain, non-school day, we found ourselves jumping and playing in the hay like young kids will do in their revelry. We finally relaxed to just lie in the hay to rest and to think.

I said, "You know brother, I have a story I made up about creation wrapped around another Greek myth (For the true version, go to Plato's Symposium). I don't know why others can't make up their own stories as well. We thrill to nursery rhymes don't we? "Jack and Jill went up the hill, to get a pail of water. Jack fell down and broke his crown and Jill came tumbling after." Two kids like us making merry! Besides, no one really knows; the story might just offer a keen insight someone else never thought about, don't you think? In my story the world was also without form, surrounded on all sides by water. In the water there lived a huge serpent. Now the Leviathan loved to eat. She ate daily twice the amount she ought. It stood to reason, if she kept doing this, she would outgrow the abyss in which she lived. Well, it happened. She got so big that she foundered on the bosom of the sea, while her back side stuck out of the waters, forming a gigantic land mass."

"That is funny", Freddie laughed. I did too.

"Just wait," I said. "Anyway, she stuck herself in the mud. She absolutely could not remove herself from the bog. On her back side she grew all kinds of vegetation from the barnacles of the sea that had attached itself to her body. Some of the crevices in her body held water where some of the fish of the deep were trapped. When the rains came, the ravines filled with fresh water, of course not in the bays alongside the sea; they stayed as they had been. Meanwhile, some found that they liked not having to live in the waters, so they stayed on her backside to become land animals. Others chose to stay because they liked a smaller place to live, preferring the fresh water to the saline mixture. Some returned to the vast waters beyond the shore, finding their way along the streams emptying into the sea. After a long period of time, there came thousands of creatures built like a ball. The odd thing about all this, they were fashioned together like Siamese twins. They had three different types. One was a dual composition of male and female. Another had two men embedded together; and the last had two women entwined. All of them clung together with two heads, four legs and arms, along with all of the other parts that are required for two people. They could walk forward, backward and sideways; and they could roll if they wanted to do so, which they did. Everyday they played the same games, right in front of her nose. They annoyed the old lady like a choo-choo running through the middle of our house. One day she grew weary with their shenanigans; in great agitation, she swatted them with a twist of her tail, tossing them as far as she could.

Well needless to say, they ended up in area now called the Middle East, Africa, Indonesia, and parts of America. In the process, they came apart. Their opposite selves got bumped in the fall. They became afraid because they saw themselves alone in a strange place. As a consequence, they started to look for their significant other. Not able to find the one who represented their exact opposite, they sought another like their former counterparts. Since they had so many of the odd balls in the beginning, each soon found a mate. The man and woman would have children, while the others would only find joy in work and mutual satisfaction."

Freddie leaned back on the hay stuck a straw in his mouth and began to talk in a very thoughtful manner. "I see what you are saying. No one really knows how we came into this world, but every thought of mankind seems to say that we developed out of the soil. It seems to me that the first man was autochthonous, that he originated from the region where scientists have found his remains; or he migrated there from a more fertile region. In any case we don't have to ask where the sons of Adam found their wives, do we? God becomes the eternal factor of life, all life. He is the ground of all existence, the unity of our lives. Thus if I am to find God, I should look within. In addition, if He is the very essence of my being, then I should try to be like Him, to discover grace, not rules that man made. It is not so much how one thinks of God, but how he lives God. To emulate Jesus means to become fully human, to immolate myself for my greater good; that is truth, love and justice. Come go with me," he abruptly ended.

We climbed down from the hay bin one log at a time. He proceeded to go to the tool shed to retrieve a shovel. I had no idea what he was going to do. After we started into the woods behind the barn I said, "Where are we going, I wasn't finished with the rest of the story." "You can finish that tomorrow," he said, "now we have a job to do." We came to a spot in the pine trees where cedars grew as well. Scattered among them were the American Holly trees where he chose the prettiest one to dig. I watched in amazement.

After this we struck for home. At the back corner of the house, facing the east, he dug a hole to plant the tree. When he finished, he announced, "This is a memorial for you and me, a kind of trinity, inasmuch as God has made us. It represents our atonement with the all giving power of the world and to the earth from which we arose."

A pristine announcement of yore,
Before the winds of time on us bore,
Here in our little garden space,
At one with nature and the human race;
Even Momma, blinded, came to see,
Freddie, me and the Holly tree.

Cain and Abel

One day in our pristine setting, Freddie and I decided to help Papa with the mending of the fence in the pasture just below the house. I had a go with the hammer; but, I didn't really want it. Freddie took his turn; he enjoyed it so much that I decided I should try to hit the staple again. Promptly, I told him that I would now take charge of the hammer. Not anytime soon would I get it. I kept pestering him until he gave it to me alright. You guessed it, right on top of my head; and it was no mean hit. I reeled. Papa took me to the house, laughing all the way. It was a good lesson for me. Perhaps the hit on my head started my madness. More than that, the hammer also signaled the soon coming end of our mythological beginning.

Fortunately, none of our spats lasted long. However, in an aside, all of them revolved around the elder brother and the prodigal son relationship. Naturally after a cooling off session, we returned to our discussions. This time we were left at home while the grownups repaired the fences. We sat outside under the huge pine tree in the front yard, me on the wagon, and Freddie leaning back on the tree itself. The story of Cain and Abel fell into place with ease after the days events.

I began, "Just outside the garden, Adam and Eve built their homestead. They had several children, the first two being Cain, then Abel. Cain became a farmer; Abel raised sheep. Now the Lord walked in the field as he did in the garden, never forsaking the inhabitants. Abel brought him fresh meat with the drippings intact. God loved Abel for his devotion. It made him happy. On the other hand, he had no respect for Cain's offering.

Cain, sensing this, pouted. On a cloudy day, the pair found themselves in a nearby field. There Cain murdered his brother out of jealousy. Later in the day, God saw Cain, but not Abel; so he asked where was Abel? Cain replied, 'How should I know; am I my brother's keeper?' Ergo, God knew immediately what had occurred. Because of this, he condemned Cain to become a vagabond upon this earth. Also, he placed a mark on his forehead to keep others from killing him."

Freddie spoke up, "Cain's question about his brother represents a universal claim on all of us. Since we all came from the same place, we have an obligation to love all our brothers, regardless from whence they came. It seems all of us have the same ancestors. We all came from some African or Eurasian stock; so, we have no right to feel superior to anyone."

Then he asked, "What do you think the mark represents?"

"Well I don't have a definitive answer, but I will give you some thoughts about what it could mean," I stated. "The first one that comes to mind is the historical view (This view comes from the banned 1st edition of the Broadman Commentary on "Genesis," by G. Hinton Davies). Legend has it that Cain is the founder of the tribe of wanderers in the land of Israel who worshipped Jehovah, the Lord of creation. They may have had a tattoo which proclaimed their allegiance to him. However, they have no concern for their brothers whom they robbed and killed at will (cf. Exodus 18; Judges 4:1). Their worship has no content; they are unscrupulously evil, while having a pious worship of the Lord with their insignia blazoned on their chest. Perhaps some of their kin might still exist today under a different banner, badges of various, pious, tangible icons, attitudes, diets or dress, non-seminal to the kingdom of righteousness.

Another theory relates to the dawn of the Patriarchal age over against the Matriarchal age (see Joseph Campbell, "Primitive Mythology"). While the former had an elaborate sacrifice system, the latter had a simple attachment to the land with sacrifices from the crops they grew. In order to cement this relationship, the writer, most certainly male, puts the emphasis on the Lord loving the fat of the firstborn animal; hence throughout the Old Testament there runs a slender thread to maintain the altar of the animal sacrifice. The Lord is shown as one who shows favoritism to the sacrifice of animals over the offering of the field. He is the absolute ruler, creator to whom man must obey. He requires the people to worship him by means of the killing of the firstborn beast. Also, he can pick and choose whom he loves, usually the younger brother. His love is conditional. This represents an earlier view of God, which would evolve later in the history of Israel to unconditional. We have to be careful we don't develop a picture of God based on man's earliest thoughts of God, spoken in various myths or understanding of ancient thought.

Therefore the mark represents a manner of worship, antithetical to the worship of the Israelites. The Canaanites were people of the soil; the Jews owned cattle and sheep. It was the same old story of the taming of the west in America, the law of the cattle and the migration of the farmer to the ranges. However, in America, the cattle association raised the beef, while the farmers grew cane. Justification of the interlopers came from their conviction that the one true God was on their side. However, neither the Canaanites nor the ranchers felt the way the intruder did. You can see the why the cauldron boiled.

Freddie laughed, "Yeah, I can see why the old men of the Bible wrote as they did. I think they purposefully wrote certain instructions to show that they were the ones whom God loved, but more importantly from the male point of view, to name their brothers and to keep women in the kitchen. The concept created a chasm between Israel and the other tribes in the area. They looked down at the 'infidels' in reproach. Quite possibly it gave them an excuse to kill and to dominate without guilt. No one can love another human if they have this attitude!"

"I agree," I answered. "Another view of the story involves the idea of God's punishment for disobedience. . . The saga continues 'the fall' story motif in that Cain would not find the ground suitable for his crops; and, that he would be a nomad upon the face of the earth all of his life. This represents man's alienation from nature, his instinctual drive; he must now find himself, his true meaning in life. It is this quest that will follow you and me. We want to know why we were born. The road will lead us as far as we are willing to go. We will have many bridges to cross, many decisions at various crossroads throughout the journey. Somewhere along the way, hopefully, we will find ourselves back in the garden. The way lies ahead through the back entrance. We will have many ideas both religious in nature and not, sometimes distinct, otherwise amalgamated. There will appear before us many ideologies as well as theologies, but we will have to pray for discernment to read the essence of each, the kernel of truth to pack in our luggage. The mark here is the offal of our existence with our hidden motives until we have learned to transcend them to true freedom. This I think is the essence of the story as well as our calling.

One other view I offer, similar in nature, before Momma calls us to dinner. Throughout the Scriptures the emphasis falls on the elder brother versus the younger brother. The idea relates to the choice of one over the other (See Myron Madden, "The Power To Bless"). One receives the blessing unconditionally, while the other feels alone and hurting, feeling unloved, having to beg for the Father's love. Unless he pleases the father by doing everything he wishes, the old man withholds love. Once a young person leaves home without the blessing, he wanders in a daze, incapable of love, feeling insignificant and worthless. Until he comes to grips with his inner confusion, he is a zombie, destined to earnestly seek love, but rarely find it. If he does, he has no capacity to give love in return. It is a selfish love which asks for more, but gives nothing in return. It makes no difference if a person happens to be female. She too has to uncover her inner tortures which can lead her to similar experiences because she lacks the ability to love and to be loved. They carry the burden along with them, the mark of Cain.

There are other ideas involving the mark like blood revenge and the writer of "Beowulf" (the reader can pull the whole story up on the internet, edited to modern English) indicated the monster Grendel came from the descendents of Cain. Probably many more ideas have been presented of which I know nothing. For now, we shall not try to go any further."

"Well I will say this," Freddie said prophetically, "Whatever the mark is, Cain went into the world free as a bird to walk the earth, perhaps never to find true freedom or fulfillment. There are many people like that in our church I'd say."

"Okay boys," Momma interrupted the scene, "Wash up for supper."

Their name is legion; they walk with a limp,
They search endlessly; they know nothing of their gimp;
E'er they wander with no bed or a lap,
Souls fed by insignificant banter and wine sap;
With many masks they prance upon the stage,
While unbeknownst the torrents of hell rage.

IN THE GARDEN

The Dream

One night I found myself in a vast pool, swimming all alone. The pool was a luscious pond in a gorgeous setting where I swam with ease. I did the back stroke, the scissors, the dog paddle and floated with ease. With every kick I heard the most delightful noise like a dove cooing; however, I could not make out her signal to me. Suffice it to say I longed to hear her tune; so the more I kicked, the louder she sang.

As the 'rosy colored dawn' appeared, the pond started to go dry. Something grabbed me. I knew how a fish felt when he is snared by a hook and pulled from his celestial fount. I fought with every ounce of my being to no avail. Out of the pool I came grasping for breath. I had been at peace with no trouble until this moment. Something took me from my security blanket to awaken me to the brilliance of a florescent lamp. I screamed in terror.

Someone handed me a key; then he guided me to a large house with many rooms and he placed me inside. On the right there sat a large safe with many drawers, all locked. I placed the key in the first box and to my surprise, it opened. In the bin I found some little pieces of cake and a few safety pins. Checking the other boxes did little good, for the key fit none. However on the ledge lay a rubber stamp with an ink pad. I had no idea why I needed those things, but the cake I decided I could use; so I began to nosh.

I tried several of the desks which were locked, but my key didn't fit. I moved to the next sealed room. My key fit the lock perfectly. I opened the door to find several pennies on the table. Not enough with which to even bother, but, I thought 'I might find some use for them.' Therefore I picked them up to put in a little sack for I had no pockets.

Proceeding on, I came to another room where again the key fit with ease. Beyond the entrance sat a mirror through which I could see all kinds of wondrous things. I stepped into the magic wonderland where I saw lambs, tigers and doves winging about in ease, singing those wonderful phrases similar to those I had heard early in the night. There came to me an alligator on whose back I rode in and out of every nook and cranny in the garden. What a privilege and delight. After the gator saw that I had grown weary, he delivered me at the next door into which I must go.

Again the key fit nicely. However, I would wish shortly that I had not entered into this room. There were two people, man and woman, who began to pull and tug at me. They tried to get me to notice this phallus attached to my body, of which I had paid no attention prior. I wanted to avoid them at all cost, thus an ensuing, desperate battle. I fought until I had no strength left. I just knew if I took that thing I would suffer greatly somehow; consenting I acknowledged the inevitable. Having won the contest, they cast me headlong into a stream of my own making toward a final door.

Here two more of the same gender, but not the same couple, grabbed me, taking my pennies to purchase my layette to cover my naked body. Another battle occurred in which again I had no chance of winning, for they were too powerful. They tossed me out the back door. I was not about to be outdone, although I was fairly certain if I got back in I would not be able to over-power the two awesome creatures. To my surprise, there was no return door; there was no key hole; there were no corners to go around to get to the front. I sat down to cry, and cry I did. When my cistern dried, to my surprise I saw a large chest nearby, which I proceeded to open.

I shouldn't have. Out popped two awesome ogres with large flaming swords trying to kill me. The battle waged for hours; at last the ugliest one raised his sword in a mighty upheaval to take me out of my misery. I just knew it had come down to very end of my existence. Ceding my fate, I lay back in resignation only to discover I had forgotten the key. I raised it in time to catch the blow of the sword. Something strange happened; I received the most joyous peace ever, with songbirds singing, to whose sounds I awoke.

To a Butterfly

Consider, if you will,
An ordinary cocoon,
Attached to a limb or window sill,
Left to the elements, to its doom?

Contrary, as we all know,
Inside, safe and sound,
In spite of heat or snow,
Till its appointed time comes around.

What once was a bug,
With many legs to crawl,
Something few would even hug,
Now it's radiant above all.

A sign of spirit and life,
And glorious dreams and hope,
Ability to overcome strife,
With strength to live, to cope.

And then the final curtain,
Can it become its best?
Of this I am certain,
To always soar is its quest!

The Explanation of the Dream

In the movie "Kindergarten Cop," one scene has a little five year old stand to make an announcement. Not knowing what he has to say, the teacher allows him to speak. He blurts out, "Boys have penises; girls have vaginas!" How poignant. At least his parents taught him the correct nomenclature for the genital organs of the male and female species. Most kids only know the terms named after the gatekeeper of heaven and an ordinary cat. One could take the gutter terms and run the gamut from there with all the sex education most kids will ever get. The four letter term for the sex act glides unimpeded in everyday language while the subject itself never gets broached in any other way.

Birth

The concern for enlightenment rests solely on the history of every human since time immemorial, with revealed truth, not old wives tales. Every birth happens in the same fashion, which includes Jesus, who was born in the same manner as you and I. (See, "Sex Without Fear", S. A. Lewin, M.D. and John Gilmore, Ph.D. Also various related articles are found on the internet). The sperm from the male orgasm carries a pair of chromosomes called "x" and "y". The ovum from the females comes to meet the traveler in the fallopian tube. Millions of sperm make the trip, but only one cell will attach itself to the egg, containing the two chromosomes, but the female only carries the "x" variety. Excess chromosomes are expelled upon merger; if not then the parent's prayer for a perfect child won't occur. If "x" meets "x", then it's a girl; and if "x" meets "y", then it's a boy.

The fertilized egg begins its journey to the uterus. There it attaches itself to the endometrium, creating a placenta. Identical twins have one placenta, while fraternal twins have two. The connection becomes the life line of the fetus, called the umbilical cord, through which the new born gets fed. The menstruation cycle of the woman then ceases because the child will use the excess materials for nourishment. The chromosomes contain the genes of each one's ancestors; in fact, they carry the genes of civilization as far back as our human race goes, hence the commonality of all humans including "Adam and Eve."

In the center of the skull and behind the nose lies the pituitary gland. Above this gland sits the hypothalamus which receives signals from the body to relay to the brain. It responds to the body by sending out nerve impulses and sometimes needed hormones. The pituitary in turn sends out some of its own. One gland called the adrenal gland receives hormones from the pituitary gland, and not to be outdone, manufactures some hormones as well to send. Its responsibility has to do with growth and development. This is the "flight or fight" syndrome we have in us. In other words, the adrenaline starts to flow.

A lack of, or too many, hormones causes birth disorders which can be traced to heredity; and they also may develop through a physical disorder. Giantism comes from excessive growth hormones while Dwarfism on the other hand, as you might expect, begins from a lack of hormones. Any of the information on the above functions of the glands has been made available on the internet simply by doing a search under the name of the gland itself.

In the same concept one can explore homosexuality. Is it not possible, given other birth defects, that homosexuality may also develop through hormone deficiency? In recent studies over the past few years, psychologists have tested several aspects of homosexual behavior. In an article on homosexuality entitled, "Facts about Homosexuals and Mental Health" on the internet, many studies have been made. Out of these came the result that many religious and bigoted people do not want to hear. They deduce that homosexuality is not psychological. In related studies on non-human species, scientists have found that among these (gulls and monkeys to name a couple) also have homosexual behavior in their societies.

One of these tests involves the sampling of identical twins where one of the twins was known to be gay. The survey shows that 52% of the other persons who shared the placenta were also gay. However in fraternal twins, only a small percentage turns out to be homosexual. Here the gene factor certainly does come into play. Can we conclude that homosexuality may very well indeed exist through natural acts and not unnatural at all? You be the judge; but, be sure to take your blinders off.

An infinite web of genes causes eye color, beautiful hair (or loss there of), facial features and etc. Does it not stand to reason that it is not unreasonable then to find biologically homosexuality comes from genes as well? I am sure that sometimes sociologically one has deep, desperate conditions imprinted on the psychic to which he or she might respond. But, who would masochistically subject themselves to such ridicule, dissociation and embarrassment that religious groups and narrow minded individuals impute. The largest conviction has to lie in the fact that homosexuality is not the opposite of heterosexuality. Hatred, injustice and scorn toward a person of such persuasion hold down the position of the opposite to homosexuality. Without further examination, any such attitude diffuses community. Whenever disrespect for another person, created in the image of God, no matter whether sexual, racial or religious, then oneness fails miserably.

If the premise remains, then it is time for the elder brothers in our society to begin to deal with the issue. One of the problems has to do with one's belief in Biblical thoughts, where tradition holds a grip on one's insight. I shall deal with this issue later, but for now, we do have deep rooted convictions which shade our minds. These take the main road of disassociation through prejudice behavior leading large numbers of people to ostracize one's brother. At any rate, it is time we begin to see the person and not his or her sexual preference. Also, the homosexually inclined person must be given the space to find their "transcendent soul" just as heterosexually minded persons ought to do. By this I mean to discover one's unique self as rendered in our embodied gender to become actualized in the flesh. A quote by Edwin Markham seems appropriate:

"Hated, despised, a thing to flout,
They drew a circle to shut me out.
Jesus and I had the wit to win,
He drew a circle and took me in."

In the process of this writing, an article appeared in "The Town Talk," the daily newspaper in Alexandria, Louisiana, dated November 29, 2003. In the article the focus of the text revolved around a discovery by scientists who identified the first gene believed to guarantee heart attacks which plagued an Iowa family. The scientists believed this break through might enable them to find other genes which lead to coronary artery disease. This supported the view held of ancestral genes present in the fetus as indicated above.

To return to the creation stories, Genesis, Tiamat and the overweight serpent all swim in the pool of oneness. Harmony and peace surround all of them until something causes disruption. In the Babylonian epic, chaos and trouble boil over in the abyss through fractured nerves, jealousy and oedipal desires. Contrast the newborn's time in the incubation period. Oneness, peace and accord preside. Upon our arrival into the world of duality, we now have fear, toil and trouble as in the pre-creation story of Marduk (Adam and Eve's eyes were opened; they were naked and afraid). The round bundles of joy are now displaced in an alien world; plus we have to distinguish between good and bad, right and wrong, sun and moon, heaven and hell, God and Satan, ad nausea. At birth, according to legend, God splits his creation into two separated halves. The altered Greek myth of creation does the same. In one case God tells Adam that Eve is his mate, to cling to her, to become one again. In the other mythological event, the male has to find his mate who was lost in the 'fall,' because he is not whole without her anymore. In these cases is not marriage, as well as the new born, a microcosm of man's ultimate search for oneness which is within him? To the former thought we shall return anon. Did not Jesus himself say, 'The kingdom of Heaven is within you' (Luke 17:12). The Greek word `evtos, (according to Kubo, A Reader's Greek-English Lexicon Of The New Testament), means exactly that, 'within you,' as written in the King James Version of the Bible.

Innate Imprints

The child will have a blend of the parents' characteristics as well from the previous generations of each family. The baby will also have some of its own as well. Instinctual behavior will be inherent, although conditioned by culture, so that the actual line to "Adam" may never occur. In fact, if one takes the Judeo-Christian trail to the garden of original sin, he or she will miss out on humanity's "reverence for life" which shows itself in every species or culture known to mankind. At the time of the child's sojourn in the uterus, he or she takes its form, only to awaken after nine months in a strange world to begin all over the process of attachment.

Tournier ("The Naming of Persons") relates man's original sin as 'reparation' of the love-communion between the mother and the child. Compare this to Fromm's aloneness in a hostile world (Erich Fromm, "Escape From Freedom"). The new born faces fear as he begins his journey to individualization. Genesis tells us, "and they were naked…and they hid themselves." We shall go further on this theme later.

Meanwhile, back in the jungle, the child in the later developmental stage of his life hears soft sounds from beyond (Paul Tournier, "The Naming of Persons") Not only does he hear the mother's voice, but he feels her heart beat and every breath she takes. He is indeed at-one with her. Here the unborn has perfect communion, perfect love. No wonder we have so much difficulty in the outside world, for at-one-ness comes at a great price. How we return to this pristine setting represents the intent of this thesis.

Tournier talks about an experiment performed by some doctors, where they used the mother's voice of a troubled child; they reduced the voice to incomprehensible words to play them to the child. They adjusted the volume up and down until it most clearly represented the voice of the mother overheard in the womb. In the following case, the child, upon hearing these words who otherwise could not talk, begins to speak. I simply relate this story to say that there are ways to regain the safety of the womb, to once again find perfect love.

If you look at the story of the child hearing the voice of his mother, you might get some insight into the phenomena of speaking in tongues. Perhaps glossolalia signifies a return to the communion of pre-birth. If so, it explains the warm feeling experienced in the event as told to me by those who speak in that fashion. It follows that the verbiage of tongues does not represent any known language because it does not communicate any intelligent idea; it only expresses feelings. These feeling bring warmth and comfort. However, they can be confused with an idea of having attained the highest degree or level of human spirituality. They can become an end within themselves, where one becomes heavenly minded, only to fail miserably in earthly relationship. As for me, I have had other experiences where I had the same fuzzy feeling without the utterances. However, we cannot build a tabernacle on this mountain nor one that goes 'even higher,' for life is lived in the valley of tears. As Willie Nelson and Ray Charles sing:

> "There were seven Spanish angels, at the altar of the sun;
> They were praying for the lovers, in the valley of the gun."

Mark 9:3 has Peter say, as he and the disciples experience the transfiguration, "Master, it is good for us to be here: let us make three tabernacles . . ." Jesus clarifies their erroneous thinking; he leads them back into the valley below where they must live.

At an Evangelism Conference some time ago the tone of the environment had a special spiritual flavor. At the end of the program several ministers had gathered to pray; they did not want to lose the spirit of the moment; more than that they knew they had to go back to the wolves and alligators; and, it would take more to live than the one moment of bliss they had received. That's the point. As bad as we need blessings, we need something intangible inside to sustain us. We do need to go to the well to drink; but just as Jesus directed his 'children' to the tangibles of one's worship, so must our soft, fuzzy moments lead us to our responsibility in the valley. More importantly, they must give us 'something more' to sustain us during the trials and tribulations of life.

On the positive side, one of the fastest growing churches in America is the church where this phenomenon occurs. It gives a person a sense of oneness to his fellow travelers and it gives a great deal of security to the person speaking the 'language.' In other denominations, the people who sit in the pew search for the same kind of experience, only they seek spirituality in a different manner. Where the tongues are spoken, there is 'built in' satisfaction guaranteed. Where they are not a part of the worship, something else has to occur or the seeker will go somewhere else; or, he will create havoc with his voice over the lack of the spiritual condition of the church. The something else involves, but not exclusive of other things, prayer, great solemnity, Bible quoting and a worship service with zing to awaken the dormant giant within.

A lady named Queen attended one of my churches some years ago. I made a statement about some people want to get "high" in church. In fact they would get so zealous that if they died they'd miss heaven completely by over-shooting the golden portals in their pursuits. I said I suspected it was not spiritual, but rather an over active thyroid gland. After church service she handed me a note which said, "Preacher, I rather suspect it is from an over active gonad!" I yielded to the Queen.

In both the tongues and the hyperactive person, the end results may lead to the belief that the means justifies the end. Also, they may assume the means represent the end. It is true that each of us wants peace, but peace will have to come through the examination of ourselves from within. Harmony with the outside world won't come in ecstatic experience, but life changing disciplines through the admonition of Jesus (i.e. love God with all your being and 'what': your fellow passenger as yourself). Just as the baby takes nine months before he comes into his own, it takes years to return to the 'garden' and no event similar to the experience in the womb is 'the zone.' I hope later to place some thoughts into the mind of the reader of times when the circumstances of creative events point to our peace in the womb, which will include the tongues experience, but not promote it; yet hopefully each event urges us to a richer life because we had those times. Simply said, these occurrences may represent the end result, but they only serve to remind us of the eschatological future which beckons us to a fuller life. They are not an end in themselves.

I have an associate of mine who told the following story:

"I had a couple to join my church some years back that was highly 'recruited' by every Baptist church in town. I thought they joined because the lady's parents belonged to our church. At any rate they came to make a significant contribution to the fold, physically and monetarily. After a period of time they began to encourage me to read a book about a nominal church member who detested tongues, but through his search for the 'Spirit,' he visited a group who practiced tongues. After his initial introduction with a spiritual guide, he found 'heaven.' My 'friends' confessed to me they had discovered this same experience. Now of course, they wanted me to have the same conditioning of the 'Spirit.' It seemed that they had searched for the most unspiritual church in our town to join so that they might, per God's instructions, enliven the church as well as save me. They chose me; or rather God directed them to me."

They could not see that underneath his exterior, bland, expression beat a heart of compassion, who in spite of all his frailties, cared about the flock as well as them. He was neither a Bible thumper nor one given to long prayers ending in sensationalism, the epitome of 'spiritualism' for them. Neither did he imbue an aura of holiness often seen in persons who think their offal doesn't stink. I always felt like those persons were more constipated than religious; or should I say, 'bilious.'

In a similar vein, I think of Mike who lived next door to me in another state. His mother was the sweetest woman I believe I ever met. She loved the Lord with all of her being; and, she exuded his love in her every day affairs, in the church and especially in her family. Mike married a young lady from another denomination, non-tongue speaking; but, they believed unless you were baptized in their belief, you could not enter the kingdom of heaven. At her funeral, still a young lady in her late forties, Mike wondered aloud, "If she went to Heaven?"

Thus mankind's quest for a 'return' begins from his alienation with a desire to reunite in the garden, (oneself), which is not one experience repeated in various circumstance, but a lifestyle in which religious happenings such as tongues may occur. Tongues, language overheard in the womb, offer only a starter kit to allow a person to see the goal of one's development toward fulfillment; whereby the function of tongues aids in an enrichment of the soil where the fruit of the spirit grows, the deep need of the soul.

It is only a short step to realize that 'desire' can become highly selfish in nature; therefore, part of the maturation factor of each individual has to do with sublimation of the ego to worthwhile pursuits. Any sense of oneness which omits the fullness of personal growth misses the mark of perfection. To make it plain, tongues and rapture in any form may or may not represent the fullness of the Spirit. The return to primordial existence features a return to at-one-ment with God, nature and one's brothers.

Every desire of mankind should seek wholeness, while not judging the path another takes.

We need eyesight which penetrates, sees beyond the norm (the traditional), eyes which think for themselves. As the evangelist says to pilgrim in his search for directions to Heaven's gate in Bunyan's, "The Pilgrims Progress":

"Do you see yonder wicker-gate? The man said no. Then said the other, Do you see yonder shining light? Keep that light in your eye…so shalt thou see the gate;…"

A friend of mind came to my house one time to visit. He had just purchased a new truck. I had never been into trucks, so when he kept calling his truck the "dually," I had no idea what it meant. I soon found out that it was in regard to the rears set of tires; instead of two, it had dual tires on each side on the rear.

In the mind we too have a "dually". It comes prepackaged with a left side and a right side. It has been made popular recently by the book, "Men are from Mars; Women are from Venus". At first blush you might think it means men think with the left and women think with the right side of the brain. However this is not always the case. How we think relates to our up-bringing and cultural conditioning. It is true though that the differences do contain mostly left and right thinking. Let's look at the chart then draw some conclusions (The internet contains many articles on this subject).

LEFT BRAIN	RIGHT BRAIN
Logic	Feeling
Fact	Imagination
Objective	Subjective
Present & past	Symbols & images
Knows object by name	Appreciates the object
Looks at parts	Looks at whole
Analytical	Synthesizing
Practical	Aesthetic
Safe	Risk taking
Reality	Spatial
Functional	Orderly

As you can see it is an over simplification to identify left brain types as logical and orderly versus right brain types as creative and unpredictable. We do draw on both sides for our personality traits. In the case of marriage, women often think more on the right side while the men think more on the left. They are programmed that way. You can see where these may come into conflict. It does appear at times men are programmed to think logically while the women think with feelings. Men seem to think practical and functional while women think orderly and aesthetically. From the right side of the brain men take risks while women think safe. In an article on the internet by Gina Shaw entitled, "The Mind of a Man," she reviews a book by a doctor who says that a man and woman are wired to think the way they do long before birth. The surge of hormones, testosterone for men and estrogen for women, engulf our brain to bring about marked differences in brain development.

In the study men seemed to give over to ideas that were analytical in nature so that they had less time to talk on the feelings level. In a PET scan, men and women were asked to do a math problem In the scan the women's brains had more light in the brain that did the men. In other words, it took more capacity for them to do the problem than men because they had to struggle more on the attempts where the men did it with ease. On the other hand, when given a sad face to ascertain, men used less capacity to perceive because they are not as sensitive; and, they spend less time trying to understand or to see without feelings.

To put this into perspective, it becomes easy to realize when a man comes home, if he doesn't care to talk on the feelings level and the spouse does, it may have something to do with left and right brain thinking. This is something each couple has to understand in order to facilitate their marriage.

Again these are stereotypes and they do not fit the mold of every man and woman. There are many men who can talk intimately while on the other hand, there are many women who can shoot a gun, mow the yard, mend broken pipes and do practical things better than some men.

Conflicts occur within the brain as the two sides disagree on the information the other one gets. The left judges desires, such as sex, where the right feels no restrictions. The left says, 'Hey, wait a minute. My upbringing says no.' It is easy to see why married adults, fellow employees and church members often disagree on issues as well. Somehow we need to reprogram ourselves so as to coordinate information. There are some "bridge-gap brains" (or middle of the road thinkers) out there that can use both sides of their brain. They can converse with the opposite sex easily; they can perceive as well as appreciate; they can also create as well as think logically. Our goal should be to find truth to set us free. Sometimes the old logic and judgment imprinted in some fashion may very well indeed be false.

In the main, our society does not use both sides easily. If there is a side that predominates, it is the left side. The common person will never reach his maximum potential because the possibilities the right brain brings to the table never receive the proper usage or recognition. Often they choose logic, reasoning and details over imagination, spatial and creative abilities. Any new idea or concept takes a back seat to hand-me-down lore, religion and customs. They don't like change; they hate those thinkers not of the fundamentalist mode, even to judge them as liberals and unbelievers, destined to burn in hell; and often they may try to help them to get there. The sin of the moderate on the other hand often shows its ugly head in harsh judgment and criticism.

As far as arguments go within the marriage, it is ludicrous to say that there will never be any misunderstandings. In fact, couples may never reach a point to where they will agree wholeheartedly on some subjects. However, most of the arguments which occur do not revolve around the issue at hand. Underneath the basic overt fight,(i.e. what started the altercation may be muddy shoes) lies the real issue involving either left or right brain thinking, or conflicts within that are from emotional scars and unholistic thinking. In order for catharsis to happen, the pair must come to grips with the real underlying problem.

Jesus' extraordinary sense of balance between his left and right brain indicates his great insight into the nature of his peers, his religious upbringing and his ability to relate both in the proper manner and at the right time, hence his spirituality. He has a remarkable sense of oneness to God and relates it to his brothers and sisters. He is kind and loving, sensitive to the weakest cry for help. He can stand firm when he has to against superior forces; and, he can turn the other cheek at the appropriate time. He has inner peace and strength which come from his relationship to God, but no doubt about from where the spirit hails; it comes from within. What one of us mere mortals would lay down our lives for our friends, much less our enemies.

> Open mine eyes that I might see,
> Insights that penetrate the night,
> As well as the dark side of me,
> A light unto my path, my plight.

Thomas A. Harris in his book, "I'm ok—You're ok", outlines three different thoughts which make up each person's life. They are parent, child and adult. In the innate exposure to the brain development discussed above, I like to use these images to further clarify the concept of left and right brain thinking. If you remember the sitcom, "Home Improvement", you will appreciate the use of the Taylor family to illustrate my point. In the

Taylor family, Jill represents the parent figure, typical left brain thinking. Tim, as you might expect, plays the role of the child, which I understand is really his comedy routine. Wilson, the faceless one, represents the hidden adult in all of us; he epitomizes the transcendent self, God in me. In the show, Wilson meets the family, including the boys from time to time, who play themselves, children, at the fence of opportunity for guidance. The writer of the show has Wilson offer an insightful truth from almost every tribe, culture or race upon this earth (Joseph Campbell spent his life on mythology around the world to demonstrate the same kinds of truths buried in other cultures). Wilson brings these truths home to the Taylor's.

Al demonstrates the purest kind of left-brained thinking. He lives at home with his mother; he wears the plaid shirts all the time; he desperately needs love and assurance, which the child in Tim rarely gives. Al can fix things with his hands which Tim can only tear up. When the scene needs a level head, Al occasionally offers adult advice, which of course Tim can't see.

Jill sets the tone for the daily functions of the family. Now when she gets out of kilter, she becomes very domineering and bossy. It sets the children, including Tim, to reeling. After she acts the "jerk", she feels awful. Parenthetically, often when we act the jerk, we don't look to see if maybe we have made a mistake or possibly come down too hard on our children or spouse. As indicated above, she acts responsibly by going to the guru next door. He always has a neat little story to tell, which leads Jill to go to the offended ones to apologize and to ask for forgiveness. The spouses then discuss the issues to find reconciliation.

On the other hand, Tim, the tool man, is cute as he goes about his merry way. Often, as his demeanor gets the upper hand, he becomes a real "jerk". There is a difference between childish behavior and becoming a child. Childish behavior results in temper tantrums because you don't get your way; abusing the rights of others; using others for your own selfish reasons; and no consideration for the welfare of another whom you are supposed to love. Childlike on the other hand is obedient to rules not because they are set in stone, but because you become a better person for obeying them; the mind of a child is the most creative element we have and we should strive to use it in our lives and in the lives of our children. Also, we need to get out to play, to let our child frolic in the chaotic world in which we live. So, whenever Tim gets out of line, off to the fence he goes. Wilson, the voice of reason will again bring Tim into focus as to what is important. The Taylor boys also go beyond their bounds from time to time to ask (if you can believe this) for guidance from Wilson.

I laugh when I hear parents say to their children, "Act your age!" I think, 'They are!' They too have to "grow up". So the parent again speaks without putting their brain in gear.

The key to our story lies in forgiveness and reconciliation. These systems of behavior lead to 'bridge gap' thinking, or left-right brain function channeled in the Spirit or adult thinking . . . Otherwise, the persons will end up being a 'jerk' all of their lives. We mainly live in and out of these two spheres. Ideally we need to find a way to use the left and right when the situation calls for it, but seek to allow the transcendent self to have the last word. We shall return to this task later.

You have seen these type persons who are very opinionated; they never listen to any other way of thinking. They wear blinders when other ideas occur; there is no gee nor haw.

I know a lady who fits this mold. She won't let her children come in the house with shoes on; they can't hang any thing on the wall; they can't play with their toys but for a little while, then they have to be put up tidily. She controls what they wear and she tells them how to think. The husband can't get a word in edgewise without getting into a major argument, which is never resolved.

You recognize the childish type also. Among other things, they feign sickness to get attention. One man I read about had trouble with his feet. He went to his doctor often without any results. Fortunately for him, his physician had the notion to have him see a psychologist. After months of counseling, he discovered he could get his way with his wife if he were sick. This was the only way he would get his austere parents to give him any attention as a child.

However, there must be a blend of the two types of thinking to which we shall return with some keys. For now just enough knowledge is given to whet your appetite toward adult thinking to overcome overactive left or right brain power. I told my wife she was an enigma. So I wrote her a poem to show her parent and her child, a blend of her personality. The truth of the matter is that we need to let our child out more often. It helps keep us out of the ruts we make. Later on I will attempt to outline some of these moments where we can romp like a faun. Now guess which part of her I enjoy the best? It goes like this:

You tell me to call, to walk and not fall;
You say answer the phone, of course with a tone,
To light a fire, as she readies to retire,
No dirt track, and the nuts crack.
Build a fence, get on the defense,

No building a wagon, kill the dragon,
Cut the grass, don't be an ass,
Take a bath, do the math.
Sensible you

Time to play, silly and gay,
Wear a hat, eat fat,
Laugh and sing, dinner bell ring,
Off to the bar, morning star.
Body so fair, sexuality bare,
Mother goose, buttons loose,
Hat askew, old desires renew,
Flavor mild, passion wild.
Insensible you

The next scenario I would like to use as my illustration, Jessie James. Growing up, Momma had a wind up Victoria as we had no electricity in the early 40s. One of the records we had was the "Ballad of Jessie James." Freddie and I played it over and over. No need to say, it was our favorite song in those days. The chorus went like this:

"Oh Jessie had a wife, to mourn for his life,
Three children were so brave,
But that dirty little coward, who shot Mr. Howard,
And laid poor Jessie James in his grave!"

First, let me use Mr. Howard. He is the character Jessie assumed to hide his real identity. He is respectable; his neighbors also considered him a very fine citizen in the small town where he and his family selected to live. Compare Mr. Howard to many today who wear no suits until Sunday.

There is a strong adherence to rules. If a person holds to certain beliefs, he doesn't have to concern himself with issues not covered under his policy. For instance, one can hold to scrip which tells no lies, speaks no foul language, does not run around on his wife, and holds to a strict code of worship in the church of his choice to cover who he really is. He wears the suit of Mr. Howard, while underneath he is a crook. He can excuse himself from his hatred of all those individuals whom he thinks God has hated as well as excuse himself for his unscrupulous business dealing; because all he has done is to have God bless his actions through prayer. If he were bad, then God would not have been 'good' to him.

When I worked for WorldCom, we had a business associate who carried his Bible everywhere he went. He would bring a devotional to the meeting just so he could be called on to put the emphasis on the Eternal One. He would read from the Bible; then he followed with a lengthy prayer to allow us to see his piousness. Afterward, he walked down the aisle with a holier than thou look which reminded me of a bloated cow. At home, he read his Bible from cover to cover. He sat in Bible study class to quote verses of Scripture verbatim. But he had a flaw. He would from time to time suppress the truth to sell our long distance service . The plain truth, it didn't matter if he hurt one of his fellow workers in the process. Of course, he bathed his efforts in prayer so God would help him to make more money. On his way to his seat, I saw what looked like an ink mark on his left temple. I had a clean, white hanky that had been properly blessed because I had been sitting on it all morning, which I intended to offer to him. However, before I could offer him my aid, I saw that the mark was a birth mark of some kind, not an ink blot at all, the mark of Cain.

One might be reminded of a scene in "Hamlet" where Polonius cues his daughter, Ophelia, to prepare herself for Hamlet, whom they try to show to the king his love for Ophelia as the reason for Hamlet's unrest. Upon Hamlet's entrance, the father hands her a devotional to read saying:

"Read on this book,
That show of such exercise may colour,
Your loneliness. We are oft to blame in this,—
'T is too much prov'd—that with devotion's visage
and pious action we do sugar o'er
the devil himself" (Act 111, Scene 1).

When I attended seminary in New Orleans, we often went to Pancho's, a Mexican cafeteria, where the food was good, inexpensive and the best part, all you could eat. On one occasion some of my peers arrived to eat. They filled their plates with large helpings. Upon arriving at their table, one of them announced, so that everyone nearby would hear, "Let's pray; Brother Bob would you lead us?" Then in an ostentatious manner, they assumed the praying hands position to pray so all could not help but see. After the prayer, they began to eat heartily. On the table was a flag where when you needed more to eat you raised the flag; upon this signal a waitress would come to assist. They raised it immediately, not waiting until they were finished, explaining to her to bring more. When she brought the seconds, they had not finished the first course but they insisted the flag remain up because they wanted her not to forget them.

When they finished, finally, they walked out, leaving no tip. I wondered if they could not see the dichotomy of their actions; also I thought of an oxymoron, "holy terror." They had a mark, alright, but it came from the proportionate amount of chili which missed their mouths to fall on the pretty white shirts they wore!

Not all Mr. Howard's are like this. Some are sincere in their efforts but believe in ritualistic codes which stifle their growth to freedom. Taco Bell has a marvelous ad which says, "Think outside the bun!" In the ad they show all the delicious foods they offer which does not come in a burger. I like to think of this as our society today. There are those who fit inside the bun. They would be what I call 'cuneiform thinkers.' Traditional values and thinking go into the make up of these heteronomous individuals or shall we say 'inerrantist.' Truth for them is etched in stone from Biblical days, held in check by our fathers, and never changes. Any idea which develops contrary to the norm is 'subjective thinking;' therefore it must pass the elders so that it might be rescued from heresy.

This kind of philosophy stems from a mind-set or principle which many believe as a consequence of an authority telling them what to think. They have a fixed system of ethics which allows no deviation. All one has to do is think this way and then there is no claim on him to do justice or mercy. They can judge another because of his religion, color or sexual preference. And in the name of Jesus kill or persecute those who are different. In the south we have seen people come who thought differently from us in regard to racial equality. We really did show them.

In the name of truth, we killed some of them. These were our convictions which we sternly believed because of some Biblical notions of God's hatred for a class of people who were "different." One can take the Bible to find any text he desires to substantiate his belief. His teaching comes from bigoted parents and/or a conservative church. So if the authorities suggest evil, in the name of conceived truth, the adherent complies? After all it is not a sin to hate what one has come to believe that God hates! If the leader said jump, they would jump. I wonder what they would have done if they could not swim?

When Ed Schmidt was commander of the VFW in Alexandria, he and several members from the post went to Shreveport for the State Convention. While there, the commander of the host post said his men obeyed everything he told them to do. Ed said, well his would too. To prove his point the Shreveport commander called two men to show their loyalty. It was the coldest part of winter, but he told them to dive in the swimming pool with thin ice layers on the top. They did. Then he asks Ed to show how his men obeyed. Ed just looked at him and said, "They ain't crazy!" In turn, the Alexandria constituents reentered the warm reception room.

Those who hold that truth comes in prefabricated parts also hold that God is transcendent, and he has spoken once and truth does not change. Herein lies part of the problem. Transcendence involves you and me. We are the ones who need to move forward. To say that the truth we hold follows Jesus has to be the biggest hypocrisy of them all when it involves hate and injustice and viciousness in the name of truth. When did we see Jesus putting a person down because he was a criminal or he was a homosexual? Or when did we see Jesus putting anyone down because she was a woman or she was a prostitute or a lesbian.

If we do this in the name of Jesus, have we not profaned the gospel? Indeed we need autonomous thinkers who can think outside the bun. If God, who is the truth, and Jesus claims that he is the truth, do we not need to ask ourselves if perhaps we have been misled by fundamentalist thinkers who refused to follow new insight? Is God buried in the past, indeed transcendent, who does not interact in the present to help us to see that perhaps our authority has been wrong all along?

Sarah Crooks in an article from the Alexandria, Louisiana newspaper some time back asked the question, 'Where did the Renaissance man go?' Well I can tell you they are available. Male and female alike represent the new-breed persons who think for themselves. They hunger and thirst for righteousness. They wear a creative hat to see beyond the milieu of mass thinking going on today. This new caliber of person does not act from the voice of an authority, they respond because they enjoy doing what they do out of a sense of responsibility to others who happened to find themselves in straits not of their making. We see the other person as one of value and worthy to love. More importantly, we do it for no reward. It is our nature. We recognize that others exist in a world of hurt and pain; and that others have experienced more pain than we have. We put compassion before orthodoxy. Accordingly, we reach out to them in love. Our motto is that we will follow new light any where so long as it is new light, counteracting centuries of witch hunts. You can read about us in the poems we write; the songs we sing; more so, you can see it in the care we give to the downtrodden who have become an object of scorn to 'cuneiform' thinkers.

Such is redemption. Truth held in conceptualizations differs from truth that has been experienced. Concepts fade when put up against convictions held that won't hold water in the face of a burning child. The kingdom calls for the Renaissance man or woman. Here we live in forgiveness. If God has loved me, then he must love my ilk, for I am the chief sinner, not Paul.

Transcendence means the purging of our souls from all bitterness and evil thought, for such do not the kingdom represent. Jesus tells us to love our neighbors as our selves. He also says to love our enemies. Now why did he have to go and say that? Romans 11:32 says: "For God hath concluded them all in unbelief, that he might have mercy on us all" (RSV).

Here is a modern day parable for our consideration:

> Once upon a time in a galaxy much like our own lived a pure colony of black birds. They enjoyed an idyllic life which was afforded to them by a generous benefactor. On certain days they would assemble to learn more about the holy life to which they were called to live. Of course, autonomous orators were not allowed to speak. They would however, take in small, frail neophytes from other flocks from time to time to teach them the way. Quite often the generosity of the holistic black birds overwhelmed the fragile vagabonds. One such little sparrow had come for a visit to see first hand of their worship.
>
> During the stay of our little Chi-chi in this pristine setting, great harm was done to another bird of her ilk that had come to visit the sparrow. It seemed the pilgrim, the sparrow's friend, was gay; and she, of all things, used a colorful expletive now and again. Her benefactors needed to purify the holy land where they lived; so they maimed the small bird while she visited her friend whom the black birds had 'taken in.' When the small adoptee contested their action, they turned on her. "How could she," they reasoned, "think differently than we do when we have shown her 'the way, the truth and the light?'" They therefore concluded the little girl bird, their protégé, would have to leave for they could not accept her questioning them. With liberty and malice to one, they soon received another to take her place. "We will give our love to the ones who appreciate it," they resolved. They had duped another orphan from afar to love and to shower with affection as shown by their master.

Contrast this parable to a poem written by a young person who had literally been tossed into the foaming sea to sink or swim. This little urchin wrote a poem entitled "Escape" to a person who had taken her by the hand:

The lonely feeling I had, I couldn't get it out of my head,
The doors were locked; I couldn't find a key.
The windows were nailed shut, with the curtains drawn.
I tried to cry out, but no one was there.
Then I thought, "There is no escape;"
But the door opened and you came walking in.
It took sometime to find you, Mom,
And you brought out the sun on my cloudy world;
Even now sometimes it rains only to make us closer!

I think you can readily see that the antics of Jessie James which has been popularized into a myth through comic books, movies, novels and simple lore represents those who do not hold to a strict form or code or creed. They allow the word of God to be put into new wine skins and then they may even take a nip without guilt or hiding it from anyone. I do not mean to infer one who thinks outside the bun is a crook by comparing them to Jessie. I simply refer to Jessie as he has been so mythologized. His life came through as adventurous to where we the reader felt he was the good guy and we did not want him to die or to get caught. In truth, we do not think we are smart nor do we think we have all the answers. More than that, we know we are not good enough! This in itself sensitizes us to our fellow passengers, our brothers and sisters.

Truth like a dagger pierces the soul,
Where tradition waves its banner on a pole;
Witch hunts and the inquisition its insignia bore,
Bearing prejudices, half truths and myths of yore!
Do we decry the blood letting?
Or do we accept the Spirit's begetting?

Meet the Parents

The reader will note that I have not said a word about Momma other than the innuendoes toward her being a traditionalist. My grandmother was one who lived inside the "bun". Her Grandpa Billings was a Baptist minister who taught the correct day of worship came on Saturday. Anyway, when Momma discovered the Seventh Day Adventist's had a congregation in our little community, she immediately joined. Our lives changed dramatically. Grandmother kept on until Papa had to sell off all his hogs. From that day forward we had no more pig meat in the house. Freddie and I had to go to church on Saturdays while all our little playmates were free. Then on Sunday, they went to church and we had no one with whom we could play.

Momma was a sweet soul; yet she mainly used the left side of her brain to act. She combed her hair the same way all of her life. Her hair was long, which she put in pigtails, then she curled them into a bun on the back of her head. She preferred fruit jars for glasses against the nice dinner ware her family had given her. Her security came from her trust in the Jesus she found in the gospel according to any preacher in her denomination. She went every week to church; she read her Bible every day scripted by reference from her church; she listened to the radio, after we had electricity, to every preacher available from an Adventist church. Everything to her was so simple. She had all the security she needed to make it through all the hard times. There were sons in the World War 11 and again in the Korean conflict. She lost two adult children to heart attacks and Papa to a natural death in his 80's. Simplicity was her lifestyle. Faith held her steady.

However, if you did not fit the mold of her belief, she had no room or courtesy toward your beliefs. She put the notion of my becoming a preacher in my head, but she expected me to be one in her church on the Sabbath day. Therefore she always felt I would see the light one day to be saved to the right belief. Also, if you ate pig meat, drank wine or any other alcoholic beverage, used colorful language, and didn't go to church on Saturday, you were doomed. She judged very harshly, causing family members to try to avoid her.

She only left Jackson Parish a few times. The one place she did go was Gentry, Arkansas. Many Seventh Day Adventists live there. An Adventist high school existed there where many people would send their children to be taught. My uncle Doug was one whom Momma sent up there, hoping they might save him where she could not. Instead he came away more confused. She took me up there also to try to encourage me to go. When we arrived it was late in the evening. I was hungry. She said don't worry; everyone up here is an Adventist. All we have to do is stop by one of these houses to tell them we are visiting and they will feed us. Well, we did, but I wasn't as sure as she was. She went in although she knew not whom they were, and returns in a few minutes with me a sandwich. I was so surprised. Even more so when I saw the morsel she brought to the car. It had two slices of bread alright, but it had been filled with a turnip green leaf!

Seventh Day Adventists teach that Jesus is coming back soon, and they have had one of their prophetesses even predict the time of his coming. When the time came and it did not happen, they had to rewrite their charts. However, it didn't deter them to continue to hold to their belief of the soon coming Lord.

Doug saw killing and grief during his time in the army during the wars mentioned above. He wondered long and hard about their teaching. He could not accept the teaching of the second coming because it did not fit into his experiences. Why would God allow such horrors when he was getting ready to return to bring peace? Doug was thinking outside the bun. Jesus and Paul did say a lot about eschatology. The early church lived in expectation of a soon coming Messiah. When it did not happen, they had to go on with their lives. The imminent end of time began to pale in the theology of the church.

It is still preached in the churches, because it has the authority of tradition behind it. But the salvation experience of the foolishness of the Gospel brings the hearer to the eschatological end. The foolishness of the cross reaches mankind through the message of Jesus' dying on the cross. The eschatological now is the beginning of eternal life, the renewing of our minds, the transcendent self born anew to live beyond left and right brain thinking. The Messianic age will not happen by an occurrence in the future. It is not predetermined by God. It happens now. We have the responsibility to respond to the call to at-one-ment to nature and to our fellow man.

One of the great needs of our lives is security to which we shall return with more later. I know countless others who love their church. Like Momma, they find their security in their church. They do not concern themselves with matters they don't care to understand. So the traditional church gives them the comfort to live in a kind of freedom. Fromm treats the concept as an escape 'from' freedom. Whatever, if they can find the security, they don't have to find answers to unanswerable questions. If their prayers don't work, they have a back up system to get by.

If they ask for something and they do not get it, they reason God knew what was best.

Momma was afraid of the dark, bad weather and especially the Devil. She would get up in the middle of the night during severe weather to get all those inside into a hall closet. All Freddie and I wanted to do was sleep; but no, we had to get up so if the wind blew the house away, we would be in the safest place. She told us tales of the mysterious, evil Satan to make the hair on the back of our neck stand up. She put scars inside of us that would take years to heal. But her Jesus carried her through all her short comings. She prevailed because she did have faith, although it was a beginner's kit. If the truth be known, however, she did more to cause us to think outside the bun than she knew or cared to do.

There were two occasions where she made an impression on me, which happened accidentally, not preconceived on her part. One day I asked her how people in dark continents who had never heard of Jesus could be saved. She turned around and picked a beautiful rose and she said, "Jimmy, they just look around. They see the heavens and this earth with all its glory. When they gaze on something as pretty as this rose, they see God. God reveals himself to them so that they might be saved." I was amazed that a bun warmer could perceive something that profound.

On occasion, I went to see her to make it a time when she was going to church. On one particular Sabbath, I arrived to take her to church. When we got to the front door she stopped to say, "Let's go back home. I forgot today is the day we have foot washing." Well I had never done anything like this, so I told her no, we would stay. The first thing the preacher did was ask for all the Seventh Day Adventists to stand. All stood except me. He knew I was a Baptist minister, so I figured he was going to have a little fun at my expense. When we sat down, he said, "Now all you who believe in the second coming stand, for that is what Adventism is about. Everyone believes that." Again I was the only one not to stand.

After the church service, as was their custom on this Saturday, they assembled in the back to do the foot wash. I gathered with them. My step father's brother looked at me and he said." I want to wash your feet." I said, "Have at it." In turn I washed his feet. I relate this story because it had an impact on me. Here in the humblest way was the scene of Jesus with his apron on, the symbol of Christianity reenacted. Poets and insightful writers proclaim this feat to those who sit in the pew. The message of the church often gets tangled in a message of success, large buildings, activity to meet the expressed needs of the people and preaching a gospel of positive thinking. Salvation becomes engrossed in four simple steps to salvation, saying the right words to be saved and then to teach them holy words to say and when to say them. The pastor meanwhile teaches them to "traverse land and sea" to make proselytes. It is a prepackaged gospel made for people inside the bun. Someone needs to say one day, "Yes it works; but is it true?"

I think the prescribed medication that the church offers today is the one thing that brought about my disillusionment. The struggle to be free moves toward something entirely different from the evangelism which is nothing more than a glorified sales pitch and bun thinking. I still have questions that no one can answer. Yet I still believe.

I often would tease my grandmother with tales to get her to think. Sometimes even she had to laugh. I told her a fictitious story where once a group of people started praying for a man with one leg shorter than the other. The more they prayed the longer the short leg got until finally it became the longest, because they didn't know when to quit. She would laugh, but she told my uncle Doug later, "Where does he get that ole stuff?" In front of Doug on another occasion, I told her out of the blue, John the Baptist was gay. Of course I knew better. I thought she was going to hit me with her broom. I thought, "Why can't the church let their heroes be human?" I knew what I said would shock her, but she just thought I was even crazier than she had imagined.

I brought up similar ideas in prayer meetings on occasion. One time I asked, "If a couple moved in next door to you, would you ask them to your church?" Of course they all said yes. Then I said, "What if you found out they lived together; they had never married. Would you invite them to church?" The answer took on different form. One lady spoke up, "I would tell them they needed to change their live style; they were living in sin!" Then she said, "After they were married, I would ask them to come." Of course, I could not resist the obvious, "Would they then want to go where you attended worship?" Her back up plan, "We are dealing with Jesus here; he will tell them to do right."

Momma died in her early ninety's. We put her in the 'box'. She had been, in spite of her fears and short comings, a source of comfort to me in my formative years, when I found myself alone in a big, cruel world. I didn't shed a tear because I knew she had finally found security and freedom. Also I knew whatever lay ahead, she had a ticket for the ride. As I passed in review one last time, I saw the mark on her left temple. I wondered why I had not seen it before; but there it was. Momma had been a burger on a bun all her life, a bird in a cage. She had not been able to soar with the eagles. Perhaps now she could.

Take your hats off to Moms,
All of you Hucks and Toms
And girls both then and now,
For she has shown us how,
To live with love and care,
Without show or fanfare,
With charity sublime,
Far surpassing her time!
She can say "Don't you dare,"
But when you hurt she's there;
When the world puts you down,
She is always around!
Thanks for your special gift;
Tho the sands of time sift,
Your song lingers on,
Long after life is gone,
Neither fortune nor fame,
But something unique, self,
Not sold across the shelf,
A legacy to last,
Til our sojourn is past,
And we walk in the sand,
Together in that land!

As a child growing up, my favorite cowboy actor was not John Wayne, although he would outlast my hero. Randolph Scott held first place; he still does. In fact, my middle son was named after him. We shortened the front name to Randal so as he would not be stigmatized by the actor. I didn't know the actor or his personal lifestyle. I only knew he stood for justice in the world in the character he portrayed. When the bad guys brought lawlessness to his arena, he set out to end the reign of terror. He was indeed my muse, a myth 'par excellence'. In 2003 Toby Keith and Willie Nelson sang a song that reminded me of all those Saturday heroes we watched long ago in the local cinema. It went like this:

"Justice is the one thing you should always find,
You've got to saddle up your boys, you've got to draw a hard line;
When the gun smoke settles, we'll sing a victory tune,
And we'll all meet back at the local saloon,
We'll raise up our glasses against evil forces,
Singing, 'Whiskey for my men, Beer for my horses!'"

Papa Norred came from the same ilk as the myths of the Saturday matinee. However, he was a real life hero. He neither had a code of ethics with no preconceived notion of right or wrong nor was he armed with bible verses to reduce others to littleness. He did what was right instinctively, living by a code, "My word is my bond." Good and evil to Papa were well defined. If he saw a poisonous snake, he killed it. If it were a chicken snake, he let it alone unless it had helped itself to some of his chicken eggs. Even foxes could roam free unless Mr. Fox decided to raid his hen house of a night. He killed his animals to eat. If he did not eat it he would not kill it; it brought a thrill to the noble gentleman to see the wild animals in his pasture; and nothing elated the old man more than to hear the freedom of the Bob White's call and the dove's coo.

He worked at the local paper mill forty hours a week. For a long time our family had no automobile so he walked to work, about two miles or more, and then home when his shift was over to put in another eighty hours on his homestead. He owned forty acres of land which he loved. You could tell it too. He fenced the whole place, keeping all the fence rows clean in the process. There were two hay meadows which he let grow so as to cut them in due time in order to provide food for the animals over the winter.

In addition, there were at least six garden spots where he grew all kinds of vegetables. Behind his barn he grew sugar cane. Yes, there was even a syrup grinder with a horizontal pole so he could hook up his mule to go round and round to squeeze out the juice. All the land was worked with a mule and a hand plow. Fertilizer came from the barnyard which was hauled by a crude slide he built, pulled by the mule.

His place was a show place. A garden grew out of the wilderness. The meadows were cleared for the cattle and the mules to have plenty of grass. The only brush allowed to grow was where the dew berry and the black berry vines grew. He had pear, peach, fig, apple, persimmon and pomegranate trees all over the place, neatly laid out. He grew a kind of palmetto bush to hang his hogs in the smoke house, when we were allowed to have them.

When hay cutting time would come, he hooked up his hay cutter to the two mules to cut the tall grass. He then, when the hay cured, hooked the mules to his rake to pile up the bundles. As children, Freddie and I would ride in the wagon to go to pick up the hay. He placed us under a large, shady oak while he and his helpers, if any, put the hay into the wagon to haul to the storage bin in the barn. They picked the Bahia grass up with a pitch fork by hand. We thought we were in heaven when we rode on top of the mass of hay in the wagon on the way to the barn.

Papa was an existential man. He was at home in a hostile environment. He had nothing but self-sufficiency to face the cruel world. His satisfaction lay within himself. All he had to do was look around at his Eden. If a problem occurred, he coped with it. If an ax handle, hammer handle or plow handle broke, he cut an oak to build another. Should bad weather come, all his animals were safe and secure inside the barn. During the night whenever a disturbance came from the direction of the hen house, he arose to face the issue. Alas, he did have to get up in the middle of the night with the rest of us should a storm hit, for Momma did not have his assurance.

The cows were milked twice daily; should one of them have a problem during the birth of the baby calf, he became a 'mid-wife' to those who experienced difficulty in the coming-out party for the new yearling. The other daily chores included feeding the chickens, slopping the hogs and tending to the needed manicure of the mules and horses. Wood was cut, often by himself, with an ax with a two-man cross cut saw, which often he manned by himself. Everything received his attention when needed, down to the winding of the seven-day clock on the mantle.

I can't leave him without giving you some of his 'non-steeple' ways. He rolled his own cigarettes from a Bull Durham pouch. Garrett's snuff, from a small tin can or a slightly larger brown jar, graced the mantle over the fireplace. Everyone, except maybe Momma, knew that in the attic over the back bedroom, a fifth of Four Roses whiskey rested for his occasional drink, straight up, from the bottle preferably. There was also home brewed beer from a huge urn, bottled and capped by Bill. Naturally Freddie and I tried it out by stealing a bottle now and again. Don't think we put anything over the ole fox, because we didn't. As long as we sampled the booze in boyish experimentation, he just grinned with an impish, yet knowing smile. Papa rarely spoke an expletive unless he and the mule didn't see eye to eye. He never attended church, but you knew he had a deep, abiding faith. It resided 'within'. Momma kept after him to join her church so he could go to 'heaven'. I think he finally conceded to appease her more than fear of 'hell' or 'dying.'

When Papa died, we put him in the box. I looked and looked, but I saw nothing on his left temple. Walking along the road which led to his old abode afterward, there was something of him in me, I knew. However, it would be a very long time before I would realize it. First I needed to eat of the 'tree of knowledge, the tree of good and evil' as seen from Momma's point of view.

The Trail

When young, I trod a well known lane,
Though rutted from some by-gone rain;
Thrills were there to behold by day,
Turtles with shells to hide-a-way,
Crickets buzzing, a song to sing,
Birds, red and blue, doves with a ring,
Then a Bob White would give its call,
While honkers flew o'er in the fall;
And no matter where I might roam,
I knew the trail would take me home.

The years before have come and gone,
The garden where seeds once were sown,
Now a horse with briars in its mane;
No traces of beauty remain,
And the way I once knew since blocked,
The gate on both ends ever locked;
Yet the old pine where I did think,
And a creek from which I could drink,
Bring to mind an insight, an ohm,
The trail I knew would take me home.

Imprints From the Magical Kingdom

In 1999 B. J. and I purchased an Appaloosa horse that we named Cheyenne. The people who sold the pony to us when she had attained her first birthday said she had been imprinted. Now, no one in our family or our neighborhood knew what this entailed. Upon our inquiry, we found that the mare had been accustomed to having human hands on her from the very first day of her life. She had no fear of a human. She loved to have someone pet her; she loved carrots and sugar cubes given to her via the hand. We had a bell which we would ring when we wanted her to come to the pole barn. Upon hearing its tone, she came running. She never balked when it rang its ap-peal.

At two years of age we began to prepare her to ride. We placed the bridal on her which was not a problem for she already wore a halter; then we placed the saddle on her which she took without a pitch. After a time, I climbed aboard. She never made a fuss about the issue. We had a neighbor's grandson ride her for two weeks to get her accustomed to her new duties, but there was not a hitch during the entire period. It didn't take but a few more rides to get her to obey completely, to neck rein and to go anywhere we asked.

Meanwhile, back in the jungle, the beat goes on, until at last it is time for deliverance from 'Eden'! The coming child will hold the memories of his coming out party in his sub-conscious mind forever, but never know them or remember them in an actual thought experience. However, they may appear in dreams disguised in some ways, which if heeded might help the dreamer to overcome many neuroses. There is a tremendous upheaval, cold, light, the need for oxygen, sometimes forceps, and separation from the mother, often declared as the alienation of communion (original sin).

As a child I had a tremendous fear of the dark. I don't know if it were associated with the birth trauma or if it came from Momma's tales of the crypt concerning ole Nick. Sometimes in the middle of the night I would awake in horror, trying to escape from some monster. Momma always said if I could call out Jesus' name I would be saved. Until I awoke fully, I tried in vain to say his name; I could not get it out I was so terrified. After I awoke, I realized it was only a nightmare.

There were many times in my life where I would experience aloneness and separation. Freddie and I were born in our own Garden of Eden, although it had multiple names. While in Texas until 1945, in the back of our house lived a couple with their two girls. Freddie and I thought they were the most fun, almost better than Santa. One day we went to play; to our surprise, the family had erected a fence around their yard. There was no gate either. We always felt they put it up to shut us out. Mother said no; but we did experience our first sense of abandonment. Perhaps it was also our first exposure of narcissism because we felt they didn't ask our permission to erect the fence?

Perhaps I should now relate the story of "Narcissus". A mountain nymph by the name of Echo loves this handsome man and she desires to have him. She comes under the displeasure of Hera, the main goddess. Hera causes her to be unable to speak unless in direct reply to a question to her by another. She can only mimic Narcissus when he talks to her. Consequently he despises her. One of the maiden sees this and wishes Narcissus would find out some day what it would be like to fall in love and receive no love in return. The avenging goddess heard; and as a result one day while getting a drink from a pool, he falls in love with his self from the image projected in the water. Narcissus is the embodiment of self-conceit. Our first impulse is to feed our little egos, hence Narcissism (See Gayley).

Shortly we moved to Jonesboro, La. It was a magical time in Beaumont which neither of us ever forgot. However the lesson of the fence would be a foretaste of the future, our coming of age in a great, big, wide world. Whether the birth trauma ever entered into our dreams, we never knew, but the cordoning us out of Eden surely did.

We played daily as before in our new home, having children nearby with whom we shared the events of the day. We rode saw horses, played cowboys and Indians and saw movies on Saturdays. On Saturday before the fall (and I don't mean the fall of the year), we went to the theater in Jonesboro. There was a different western hero every week coupled with a cartoon and a serial that kept you in suspense until it ended in ten or so weeks. There were Randolph Scott, Hopalong Cassidy, Gene Autry, Roy

Rogers, Jimmy Wakely, Johnny Mack Brown, Lash Larue, The Durango Kid, Red Ryder and Little Beaver, Gabby Hayes, Frog Man, Fuzzy St. John and John Wayne, to name a few. These people gave us fodder for our escapades throughout our garden days. They also provided our theological training, only we didn't realize it at the time.

The state fair occurs every year in Shreveport, Louisiana. Now Freddie and I have visions of one day getting to see the famous cow named Elsie. We are believers in fairy tales; this one says Elsie produces chocolate milk. We go about ten or fifteen miles when our excitement turns to sorrow. Both of us begin to feel sick. Well, Mother turns the car around to take us to the doctor. Of course, we protest to no avail. We are sick and we are upset. The two maladies make matters worse. We never find out for sure our illness or at least, we don't remember, but the doctor treats us to two ordeals, a shot and no trip to the fair. The second big disappointment of our young lives happens on this fateful day. Again, Paradise begins to fade.

Whether Freddie and I knew about the unrest in our home, I don't know for sure. I do know that Mother and Dad slept in a huge wooden bed in which we were not allowed. It represented safety and security to us. One night Freddie and I sensed something wrong. We had no idea what? Therefore we leaned on our aunt to let us sleep in the big bed, the one off limits. She gave in. I don't ever recall feeling as secure as I did that night.

That fateful night, Mother and Dad separated for good. We only saw him maybe four times until we were at least 17 years old after that. We moved to our last garden spot, Norred Hill. Momma and Papa, whom I introduced earlier, provided us with much love and attention. We grew even more attached to our mother. In secret, we were glad to have Dad out of our lives. This meant we had Mother to ourselves. Here is where ole Oedipus reared his ugly head for the first time. She spent more time with us on her days off than we had seen before. Her lap was a very, rich comfort zone. In no time Freddie and I began to discover the luscious land to which we were now a part.

Until around 1948, we had no electricity, running water or butane. This meant wash tub baths, porcelain urns, outdoor toilets, wood cook stoves and coal oil lanterns. Oh yes, don't forget the Sears Roebuck wish book. Saturday night baths were fun if you were the first to go in, otherwise you didn't need soap by the time you bathed. I guess you can say because of the outdoor facility, Freddie and I were very anal retentive.

In the area where we lived, we rarely saw snow. Around 1946, it snowed heavily. Freddie and I played all day, making snowmen, throwing snowballs, with Momma right out in the middle of it all. Mid-afternoon, she told us to bring us in some snow, which we did for she said we could have some snow ice cream. I don't believe I have ever tasted any thing as good as her snow ice cream. Freddie agreed. I had no idea how she made it, and until this day I still don't know. We were too enthralled to find out her recipe; I have often wished I had paid more attention to their homespun knowledge.

A typical day in wonderland occurred each morning we awoke unless we had to go to school. We played our games; we slid down a huge hill on card board boxes we shot at black birds with our Red Ryder B B gun. A nearby store sold 5 cent sodas where we went quite often. We built log cabins; we stole grandpa's home made beer plus we had four swimming holes, a pond, a trestle, Dugdemona Creek and the creek in front of the house. At night it was off to bed to talk for awhile before sleep encompassed us.

Christmas was always a magical time for us. Momma filled up our red wagon with all sorts of nuts and a variety of candy bars. Cedar trees grew in abundance, so all we had to do was find the one we wanted. Among the trees grew Holly, which Momma used to decorate the house. All kinds of goodies, not to mention the Santa gifts, came our way on Christmas day.

Our training included a relationship with a number of black people in those days. Because of these people, Freddie and I were never deeply prejudice. Momma had us call them aunt. They came each day and in exchange Momma gave them butter, eggs, milk, clabber and meat from the cattle Papa raised. Aunt Finny's husband and Papa helped each other out when extra work needed to be done, like when hay season came. Freddie and I wanted a dog; the old black man had a bull dog for which Papa traded to him an old mule. The dog had the mange; and the old mule was about dead. Each thought he had gotten the best deal. Papa dunked the grey dog in a vat of oil which cured his mange. The mule died three weeks later.

By 1948 we had propane gas, electricity and running water. Of course, the telephone came too. Our lives changed somewhat after these events. Electricity meant we could have a radio. The radio brought 'B Bar B' from Del Rio, Texas, 'Amos and Andy', 'The Shadow Knows', Seventh Day Adventist preaching, 'Jack Benny' and the 'Grand Ole Opry' into our bed room. We thrilled to the adventures of all our radio heroes, but not the preaching. I include this bit to say we had our understanding of God fashioned more through country music, fairy tales and western movies than the preacher on Saturday scaring the "hell" out us.

Our red wagon was a solace to us. It was a church, a cab and an escape vehicle. When we sat in it to ponder religious questions under the pine tree it became a church. We had the wagon with us in Beaumont where we hauled (and were hauled) the neighborhood children around. It fulfilled the same function at Momma's. For whatever reason, one day Freddie had me pack up a change of underwear and a couple of sandwiches. He thought we should just run away. I liked the idea; in no time, we began the journey to the end of the dusty road. After crossing the bridge, we saw Mother and Papa coming down the paved hill. Actually we were relieved because we felt sure they would tell us to get home. They didn't. They laughed; and they continued on their merry way. Well, we thought about it for a while; then we scampered back to our security blanket. The wagon had become a cab again, for Freddie rode in the wagon while I pulled him home.

Mother soon started dating our future step-father. When she left to go on a date, Freddie and I would sit at the window watching them until they crossed the bridge in front of the house, screaming as loud as we could, because we wanted to go to be close to our mother. We felt abandonment. The biggest reason was because we didn't want her to have anyone else. We knew we were losing her.

The final, gut wrenching fear came in 1949 when Mother remarried. They hauled us off the farm to live in "Egypt." It was the end of Eden. Our security blanket had been tossed out. A barrier prevented us from an entrance. I would get to return; but Freddie never got the chance.

As children, we never understood our step-father. He was an austere man who didn't know how to show love. In all the years we lived with him as children, he never once took us on his lap to encourage or show affection. He knew how to use the paddle or his belt however. Through the years Freddie and I sought to buy his love by giving him various items we had, like tools, for instance. We felt like we needed to please him in some way. Also, our complexes kept us in trouble with him until we were grown. Things were black and white with him. He didn't understand emotions and inner needs very well.

They never knew we had an Oedipus complex; we certainly didn't either for a very long time. I don't think Freddie ever knew. It would be years before my step-father ever really saw me as a person and not judge me by my outer actions which stemmed from inner, emotional problems. In time I would get beyond the rough exterior to see the inner person of both him and me. After we were grown, we learned to appreciate him.

Actually, our new benefactor was good to Freddie and me. He always kept us fed, clothed and a roof over our heads. He made sure we got a good education, although Freddie would drop out at his own choosing. I think it was love. I started to college with the new parent's help because I had no one else. I loved him a lot in spite of the resentment in the early years. I needed love and a kind word. He, of the old school, thought what he did expressed his feelings. It came to mean that through the years. I think he had to prove his worth to his dad also. Perhaps he never did. Maybe just a hunch, but I believe I am right.

O Tanager

In this vale of tears,
Where evil awaits to steal the soul,
I first saw my Isoldt, her bed of crystalline,
To only see but not touch,
Where the Tanager sang her sweet song.
Beowulf in search of Grendel,
Then to pursue the legend of the lost,
Yet still bourn a visitor in the noble heart,
Yon fair maiden's grotto,
Where the Tanager sang her sweet song.
Dragons slain, damsels rescued,
Orthodoxy replaced by the quest of the chalice,
Tho haunted by visions in the night,
Of a love on which dreams are made,
Where the Tanager sang her sweet song.

Freddie developed diabetes around 10 years of age. The doctor put him on insulin right away. He would suffer greatly from this malady which eventually led to his death at the age of 29, early in 1971. Freddie didn't fit into any of the modes of the mark of Cain I knew. I looked; he did have a small smudge on his left temple someone had inadvertently placed there. I put my hand into the box to gently wipe it away. He left behind three precious girls and his wife.

I visited the old home place where the house still sits in 1999. The Holly tree that Freddie planted had been broken in half by a heavy wind storm and the tree top had fallen through the roof into the bedroom where Momma slept before her death. The once pretty, garden grove now lay fallow, all in disarray with trees and scrub brush growing where lilacs once bloomed.

I ran across this poem while writing this story and I thought of him. It was written by J.R. Lowell (I am grateful to Gayley for providing this poem for me).

61

The Shepherd of King Admetus

There came a youth upon the earth,
Some thousand years ago
Whose slender hands were nothing worth,
Whether to plough, or reap, or sow.
Upon an empty tortoise-shell
He stretched some chords, and drew
Music that made men's bosoms swell
Fearless, or brimmed their eyes with dew.
Then King Admetus, one who had
Pure taste by right divine,
Decreed his singing not too bad
To hear between the cups of wine:
And so, well pleased with being soothed
Into a sweet half-sleep,
Three times his kingly beard he smoothed,
And made him viceroy o'er his sheep.
His words were simple words enough,
And yet he used them so,
That what in other mouths was rough
In his seemed musical and low.
Men called him but a shiftless youth,
In whom no good they saw;
And yet, unwittingly, in truth,
They made his careless words their law.
They knew not how he learned at all,
For idly, hour by hour,
He sat and watched the dead leaves fall,
Or mused upon a common flower.
It seemed the loveliness of things
Did teach him all their use,
For, in mere weeds, and stones, and springs,
He found a healing power profuse.
Men granted that his speech was wise,
But, when a glance they caught
Of his slim grace and woman's eyes,
They laughed, and called him good-for-naught.
Yet after he was dead and gone
And e'en his memory dim,
Earth seemed more sweet to live upon,

More full of love, because of him.
And day by day more holy grew
Each spot where he had trod,
Til after-poets only knew
Their first-born brother as a god.

OUTSIDE THE GATE

The Key

"When Jesus came into the coasts of Caesarea Philippi, he asked his disciples, saying, whom do men say that I am? And they said, some say that thou art John the Baptist: . . .
He saith unto them, But whom say ye that I am? And Simon Peter answered and said, "Thou art the Christ, the Son of the living God.
And Jesus answered and said unto him, Blessed art thou, Simon Bar-jona;
For flesh and blood hath not revealed it unto thee, but my Father which is in heaven. And I say unto thee, That thou art Peter, and upon this rock I will build my church;...And I will give unto thee the keys of the kingdom of heaven: . . From that time forth began Jesus to shew unto his disciples, how that he must go unto Jerusalem, and suffer many things of the elder and chief priest and scribes, and be killed, and raised again the third day. Then Peter took him, and began to rebuke, saying, Be it far from thee, Lord: this shall not be unto thee. But he turned, and said unto Peter, Get thee behind me, Satan:. . . Then Jesus said unto his disciples, If any man will come after me, let him deny himself, and take up his cross, and follow me. For whosoever will save his life shall lose it: and whosoever will lose his life for my sake shall find it. For what is a man profited, if he shall gain the whole world, and lose his own soul? Or what shall a man give in exchange for his soul? (Matthew 16:13-26 KJV)

At first blush, it appears Jesus gives the authority of the sacramental church to Peter. Actually, he gives his disciples the ethical and spiritual behavior to live here in this world. Transcendence is to be lived out in this world. The key is found when Jesus tells those followers it is not enough to love your ilk; they must love their enemies as well. Later he tells a scribe the greatest commandment is 'to love God with all your heart, with all your soul, with your entire mind, and with all your strength; and the second is this, you shall love your neighbor as yourself.' (Deuteronomy 6:4; Leviticus 19:18). It doesn't get any better than this, nor clearer.

I had a couple who wished to discuss the Bible with me one day in my office. In fact, they came to instruct me in the truth, to help me become more spiritual. Their illustration was typical church oriented spirituality. They claimed if they attended church, read their Bible and prayed earnestly they would, like Moses, live to have a ripe old age. Moses lived a long time and when his days on earth was over, God took him home, as he has no grave site. They had recently been involved in an all night prayer meeting for one of their elderly relatives, who now was in recovery because of their earnestness. Just for clarification, she did live a few more months, and I doubt it was because of the prayers, no matter how earnest they were. At any rate, the next year the same type of action was taken for someone's mother who was dying of cancer. She had no reprieve. I wondered why their prayers had obviously failed, (not enough faith, did not pray long enough etc).

I related this story to show how we can take things out of context, to run with the bulls, never realizing sooner or later they will gore you. Moses, like Peter, never really got the story straight. Moses never reached the land of milk and honey. The reason he didn't was because of his arrogance and temper. He showed contempt by striking the rock to get water for the people (Numbers 20:11). The land of milk and honey was never the land of Israel; it was within. He just didn't get it. Peter never got it either. Nor will we if we rely on external things.

I have a friend who sent his daughters to a 'Christian' school. One day he says to me, "Jim, my daughter can quote the entire 1st chapter of John." He brings her in and sure enough, she can. I wanted to say, 'Ok now tell me what it means in terms of your life;' but I didn't.

We cannot get a guarantee on the number of days we live, but we can get as close to heaven as we can get by learning what it means to lose our lives to gain the kingdom through the key to which we shall now move. Why is it we build so many sand castles on half-truths while the very words and life of Jesus are placed on a back burner to our fickle proof-text proliferations?

In my first church, the pianist got her feelings hurt over some minor altercation. She quit church for three or four weeks. Guess who got the brunt of her ire? The preacher received the venom. After about three weeks, I decided that I had had enough. I stopped in her home where her husband let me in without any trouble. When she saw me, she ran toward me saying, "Oh, Jim, I am so sorry." You see the dust had begun to settle.

We can be full of it; or we can be full of the spirit. The Bible tells us in the beginning, man was created from the dust of the ground; God then animated him by placing his Spirit within. It is up to us to choose which one will rule our lives. We can continue on in our left-right brain usage or we can choose to think with both sides, moving toward "bridge-gap" thinking.

To a Rose

Roses live out their lives in exquisite beauty,
Not because, as their species, it is a duty;
It is but the very essence of what they are,
Bestowing their elegance like some far off star,
Illuminating our realm of drear existence,
Maintaining a sweet fragrance in ever instance,
Saying poetically without a spoken word
Gentle thoughts of the heart which clamor to be heard.

Every new morning may they brighten your day,
Emitting hope for you in a shiny array,
And after they are gone, may their meaning linger,
Like love songs remembered by a gifted singer,
Music that says I am so glad we had this day,
And which says that someone cares in this minute way;
For the flowers speak of your beauty beyond strife,
And like the rose, you heighten each day someone's life.

The Temptations

In 2003 I had the opportunity to participate in the study "40 Days of Purpose". Rick Warren's book, "The Purpose Driven Life", provided the impetus for the program. The first memory verse we learned came from Ephesians 2:10 quoted from the NIV Bible. "For we are God's workmanship, created in Christ Jesus to do good works, which God prepared in advance for us to do." The author said we 'were born by His purpose and for His purpose.' In other words, his play thing? Later Warren proclaimed we were created to make God happy. Now, if we didn't make him happy, could we expect him to drop a coconut on our head? From what I've seen, it appears mankind created God to make themselves happy. The whole idea seemed to promote one's life in the church, to make him a better church member. The purpose driven life had the following ingredients: worship: "You were planned for God's pleasure;" fellowship: "You were formed for God's family;" discipleship: "You were created to become like Christ;" ministry: "You were shaped for serving God" (this by the way is in house ministry); evangelism: "You were made for a mission" (out of the house).

Each of these things has good qualities. The intent is good, but I saw in the study groups the direction the impetus went. That's just it! The simplicity of it states if you can do them, you will know the purpose for your life. Finally, what about those who do not see the need for church? Are they missing the boat? The word in the Bible verse 'workmanship' comes from the Greek word which means, poem. Have you ever read a beautiful poem which struck you as having significance? Poets today are more than simple. They are complicated individuals who strike at the structure of 'green house' thinking. They use metaphors to question the logic of institutional thought. They put their fingers on the issues of this troubled world to let us know their pains and how they cope. Mostly, they say we don't have a clue as to what the answer is. We look for God; and he is in hiding. We can strike the trail to him, but we never, ever have him in our grasp. We are his poem, not his puppet; we can challenge and we can disbelieve if we want. And guess what? God is not unhappy one iota.

We do have family, but we rather pick and choose. If we are serious, then we have to learn to love everyone because we are all created in the same pod. Our differences ought to make us more sensitive to each other. Instead, it divides. What occurs within the 'family' has more to do with 'spiritual bigotry' than love. Here a person feels comfortable in his church which meets all his needs. His church is the biggest and best and most spiritual in the whole town. They often look down their noses at smaller churches as well as other denominations. Somewhere along the line they need to ask themselves if their membership is the essence of their commitment?

As far as ministry goes, it is a way of life, not just toward our fellow church members. That we ought to do, but not forget that everyman is our brother which calls for compassion. So much of our work today is more 'spiritual masturbation', non-seminal activity rather than love and concern. Our church used to go to the nursing home to sing and to preach the gospel. One of the things I noted, we always could be sweet and attentive to the residents; but we were superficial because we never took the time to find out who they were or from where they came. There can be no real ministry without intimacy. It is one thing to carry the bread and wine to them; it is quite another to feel their pain and sorrow.

One young girl came home late from school and her mother demanded to know why. She replied, "My friend Kathy's doll broke on the way home." "Well did you fix it for her," the mother replied? "No, Mother, I held her hand while she cried." Touché!

I called a friend of mine in another town one Sunday morning before church. His wife answered the phone to tell me that her husband had already left for the church house. We chatted for awhile before I said, "I am thinking of quitting my preaching job to go into the real ministry like Mother Theresa." Well her reply came very quickly, "You better quit that foolishness and get back in that Bible!"

Now where have I heard that before? A prescribed format precludes our understanding to where it blinds us to reality, or at least to other methods of behavior. Also judgment of another denomination or person promotes stereotyping, discrimination and prejudice thinking.

And evangelism! What in the name of God is going on? While studying this section in the forty days of purpose, one sweet lady says, "I just can't go door to door to try to get people to come to my church. I suppose it is because I hate for the Jehovah Witness people and the Mormons to come to my door to evangelize me." I told her it is not that we are directed to go into the world; it is as we go that our little light may shine so that others might see compassion and kindness in us. True inner beauty, the poem in action, does more than someone armed with the four spiritual laws.

Evangelism sometimes takes on the character and influence of the elder brother vs. the prodigal brother. In the eighties, I visited a church in New Orleans where a revival was in session. The Preacher was one who was a professional Evangelist. He railed hard against the sinners. He talked down to the congregation to let them know they had sin in their lives. Also he cut loose on all homosexuals, drunks, overbearing men and women, couples living together not legally married and divorcees. In order to get their lives straight, to make God happy with them, they needed to repent to be baptized right now. Then he proclaimed, tomorrow night I am going to give my testimony, so be sure to be here.

Well, the next night he began to tell us how low down and dirty he had been to the point of making it seem attractive. Luckily God let him live to be saved. God finally found him living in such a disgustful manner to call him from his wicked ways to preach the Gospel. Right then and there he answered the call to righteousness. He hated sin in any form because God hates it. Now he proclaimed how good he was. "My, my," I thought. "He had just painted a picture of a spiteful ole man who was nothing like the prodigal's father." Yet he went on to say, if you are remorseful, the Father will be quick to forgive. Didn't the father in the elder brother story see his son coming from a distance? How could he know he had remorse?

I rather suspected our evangelist had fashioned a little box (or bun) in which he could squeeze to excuse his real fears and inner demons. His missiles of destruction about hell seemed to bring him a great deal of delight. I could not help but feel sorry for the poor unfortunate ones who were doing the best they could to make it from day to day without having to be ashamed of their lifestyles, destined to burn unless they accepted his God. Can you imagine a young girl who had a baby out of wed-lock sitting there feeling already like God doesn't love her because her parents don't, and now this?

In the late seventies or early eighties, the churches of Rapides Parish, Louisiana, went together to sponsor a Billy Graham Crusade. Billy would not come but one of his top aides would take the preaching assignment. It turned out that he had had heart trouble; therefore he could only do the preaching each night. He creped to the podium each night, then as if God flicked the light, he preached with amazing strength. After about 30 minutes or so, he would say, "I have to quit now, my strength is all gone."

He exited in the same manner in which he arrived. One thing he made sure we heard. He was there to preach to the lost to bring them to justice. It would be better to accept the Lord early to give your life and soul to God. He told of an elderly man who had been saved. He said his life and deeds had not been lived for the Kingdom but his soul was saved for eternity. I could just hear Satan saying, "Lost another one to the guy in the white hat!"

This past year, 2003, I heard a lady minister preach on 'sin.' She proclaimed sin to be evil. We need to change from sin to a life of goodness. Sin destroys and goodness builds. Sin is destructive. Sin separates us from God. On and on she went. Later in a Sunday school class, one member said we really needed more sermons like that. Again, my mind wondered, "What sin did she have in mind?" Does anyone ever say," Hey, no matter what you do, I love you." You may have problems; so do I. Let's walk hand in hand together through this.

My Dad abandoned Freddie and me when I was six and he was four. We saw him rarely after that and he never paid any child support or offered any money to Mother and Harry for any reason. I could have hated him; I understand my Mother for having a bitter taste in her mouth over him. Yet, B J, my wife, and I were the only ones in the world who said, "Hey, it's ok, we still love you in spite of the past." I could have avoided him as he did us, but instead I heard a different drummer; it turned out to be very beautiful music. I looked on the inside, not the exterior fluff which controlled his life.

Written to Pop With Love

I watched him over the years,
Never able to overcome the fears,
Talented as his father before,
Limited in scope, and could do no more,
Therefore lived in crippling self-doubt,
Causing little joy out and about.

He loved his father as did you and I,
And longed to see him, and hoped by & by,
To walk along and talk of an old day,
When life was happy, free and gay;
He looked to me as his guru,
And hoped I could pull a miracle or two,
I told him I didn't know the way,
But we'd walk together each and every day.

I read the above poem (there's that word again) at his death; but I added a line from Wordsworth's, "The Solitary Reaper":

> "Whate'er the theme, the maiden sang
> As if her song could have no ending;
> I saw her singing at her work,
> And o'er the sickle bending;
> I listened, motionless and still;
> And, as I mounted up the hill,
> The music in my heart I bore,
> Long after it was heard no more."

Oh yes, he wore the mark. His mark came from the repetition of making the same old mistakes over and over again. He was set in his ways; he always had the same ideas, never wavering. Loneliness was his lot. He was free, but never knew real freedom.

> And in Luke 4:1-12 we read:
> "And Jesus being full of the Holy Ghost returned from Jordan, and was lead by the Spirit into the wilderness, being forty days tempted of the devil. And in those days he did eat nothing: and when they were ended, he afterward hungered. And the devil said unto him, If thou be the Son of God, command this stone that it be made bread. And Jesus answered him, saying, It is written, That man shall not live by bread alone, but by every word of God. And the devil, taking him up into a high mountain, shewed unto him all the kingdoms of the world in a moment of time. And the devil said unto him, All this power will I give thee, and the glory of them: for that is delivered unto me; and to whomsoever I will I give it. If thou therefore wilt worship me, all shall be thine. And Jesus answered and said unto him, Get thee behind me, Satan: for it is written, Thou shall worship the Lord thy God, and him only shalt thou serve. And he brought him to Jerusalem, and set him on a pinnacle of the temple, and said unto him, If thou be the Son of God, cast thyself down from hence; For it is written, He shall bear thee up, lest at any time thou dash thy foot against a stone. And Jesus answering said unto him, It is said, Thou shalt not tempt the lord thy God." (KJV)

The temptations of Jesus offer us a clue as to the deepest needs of our lives which play an active role in the way we live. More often than not, we never know why we act the way we do. I am not trying to be an iconoclast when I offer an alternative to much of the preaching in the church today. I am, however, trying to show perhaps the direction might need different signs. As Yogi Berra says, "When you come to a fork in the road, you gotta take it." While that is funny, on the serious side, when the Knights of the Round Table of yore came to the forest, they cut their own trails through the trees. Perhaps it is time for modern man to blaze a few trails by thinking outside the "bun."

The first temptation involves hunger or pure economics. To put it another way, one of the deepest needs in our lives comes from our first fear of the new world as we enter it from the womb. It implies a need for security. In mine and Freddie's case, we have several events in our young lives to cause our deep need to engulf us. Adam and Eve are naked and afraid. Fromm and Tournier have told us earlier fear and desire come into play in our early lives. And so they do.

"A chicken in every pot and a roof over every head" won't cut it. Insecurity goes deeper than that. You will recall Satan's inquiry to God about Job, "Will a man serve God for naught" (Job 1:9)? Jesus says security goes deeper. If you look at the story of Job, you will see that all he lost, God gave him back even more. The response today requires God give us more. It appears what we have is God turning the stone into bread in order to answer our prayers. Jesus does say, "Whatever you want, ask, seek and knock." If you read on you will discover he means if you want more of God then ask, seek and knock and it will be given to you.

The church has been a haven for many through the years. The Catholic Church has really been a source of blessings to countless millions. Those individuals who follow these paths have a great deal of security. They are to be envied for their sincerity and devotion to their church. Their simple faith brings them much happiness and joy. No wonder the Protestant Churches look in amazement at them because they are so free to live a life without all the restrictions that their denomination places on them. Especially those churches that don't believe in drinking, dancing or holding services at any time of the week look askance at those who do these things in the name of religion. Let it be said, however, if a person desires not to dance or drink and wishes to attend church at 11 A.M., they have the right to do so. They too have security in their abstentious behavior; and they have the right to their beliefs. Now if they claim they don't, and they slip around to do, that is entirely another matter. Wherever we find security, we must not impose our beliefs on another, for when we do, the family of man disintegrates.

Nathaniel Hawthorne, in his book, "The Marble Faun", tells us about Hilda in her discovery of the Catholic Church. Hilda had a terrible burden not of her own making. She had seen two of her best friends commit murder. She never told anyone her story. It weighed heavily upon her, changing her from the dove-lady to one estranged from nature and people. She lived in Rome where the cathedrals abounded and mass could be held at any hour. She was impressed with the convenience of the Catholic religion to its adherents. He wrote:

> "In the hottest, fever-fit of life, they can always find, ready for their need, a cool, quiet, beautiful place of worship. They may enter its sacred precincts at any hour, leaving the fret and trouble of the world behind them, and purifying themselves with a touch of holy water at the threshold. In the calm interior, fragrant of rich and soothing incense, they may hold converse with some saint, their awful, kindly friend. And most precious privilege of all, whatever perplexity, sorrow, guilt, may weigh upon their souls, they can fling down the dark burden at the foot of the cross, and go forth—to sin no more, nor be any longer disquieted; but to live again in the freshness and elasticity of innocence." (pg.287)

Hilda did find relief for her troubled spirit by going to confession. However, she comes from Puritan stock, as Hawthorne himself was. The Priest hears her confession while knowing she is not of the true church. He comes to her afterwards to try to bring her into the fold, to which she refuses. She tells him she will be eternally gratefully and one day when they meet in heaven, she will remind him of her thankfulness. She refuses to be drawn into the "bun".

Earlier the author of this novel had indicated that there was more to security than meets the eye. He said of Hilda's plight:

> "Had the Jesuits known the situation of this troubled heart, her inheritance of New England Puritanism would hardly have protected the poor girl from the pious strategy of those good fathers. Knowing, as they do, how to work each proper engine, it would have been ultimately impossible for Hilda to resist the attractions of a faith, which so marvellously (sic) adapts itself to every human need. Not, indeed, that it can satisfy the soul's cravings, but, at least, it

can sometimes help the soul towards a higher satisfaction than the faith contains within itself. It supplies a multitude of external forms, in which the spiritual may be clothed and manifested; it has many painted windows, as it were, through which the celestial sunshine, else disregarded, may make itself gloriously perceptible in visions of beauty and splendor. There is no one want or weakness of human nature, for which Catholicism will own itself without a remedy; cordials, certainly, it possesses in abundance, and sedatives in inexhaustible variety, and what may once have been genuine medicaments, though a little the worse for long keeping (pg.279) ."

I belonged to the VFW when I first met George. I have met many good folks there, some of whom belonged to a church, some of whom did not. George did not, but we struck a chord. He accepted the fact that I was a minister in the 'lounge' without any judgment; and I took him at face value, accepting him as a person of worth and value. He asked me to do his funeral service when he died, as did countless others. I agreed to do so. Before long George passed away; his family, because of his making known his desire to have me do the funeral, called to ask me to participate. Before George died, for some reason or other which is beside the point, George had undertaken Catholicism. They told me the Priest from the Catholic Church would do the funeral, and since I wasn't qualified to stand in their pulpit, they wanted me to do the graveside service, to which I accepted.

At the service in the church, the Priest told how he had visited George for many days to prepare him for inclusion into the church and to receive his first communion. He had brought the sacrament himself to George and he partook. Because of this, he assured the faint hearts that George had been received into glory. From this high moment, we go to the gravesite where I took over. I told them, with the Priest there to hear, about Nathaniel Hawthorne's struggle with his own religion. He apologized to his peers and to his readers for centuries to come for his own family's behavior in the shortsightedness of the Puritans as portrayed in "The Scarlet Letter." Later in his life, he went to Rome where he became enamored with the Marble Faun of Praxiteles, a production of a baroque society. There they lived, danced, laughed and celebrated the festival of Bacchus. They judged not nor did they concern themselves with the religion of another. I told them how George and I viewed the other. To me, George was like a faun, albeit in retreat. Then I related to them how I thought George's entrance into the heaven went. I said, "When George arrived at the gate, there were so many expectants that he had to take a break in a large room assembled like a saloon. He went to the bartender to get his ticket for his entrance through the gate. The bartender told him it would be 1 million dollars. George stood agape as he felt, like Sarte, that he had "become as a traveler without a ticket." One of the visitors seemed to be different from the others; he was more like a greeter than a pilgrim. He arose from a rear table to get the ticket agent's attention to say. 'It's okay Pete; put it on my tab.'"

Afterward, one of the daughters said to me, "Now I know why my daddy wanted you to preach his funeral." In the final pass and review, I saw the mark on his left temple. It had been put there recently by some unknown hand. Perhaps George had a fear of death and he took out some insurance, the blessing of the Catholic church.

Jesus' independence placed him outside the current religious concepts of his day. He still went to the synagogue to teach, but his security came from within. He challenged the ideas of his day. He sought to replace "herd thinking" by calling men and women alike to find for themselves independence. He was indeed an existential man alone in a hostile world. No one understood him, much less his mother. He certainly did not get any understanding from his closest allies. His answer to Peter in the Scripture from the chapter on 'The Key' implies his encounter with the tempter, "Get thee behind me Satan."

Today as well, we have spiritual dependence. We depend on someone or some group to guide us. When will we ever come to understand religion does require introspection as well as an objective mind, open to new truth. In addition we have to learn to try to see another person as having that same right. Whatever they believe may hold some measure of illusive truth. If it does not, they have the right to live it, not to judge anyone else for thinking and acting differently. Difference in opinions takes Jesus to the cross. Anyone who thinks outside the 'bun' can expect the same treatment unless understanding, acceptance and a desire for relationships enter into the repertoire of the heart of those inside the 'box.'

True freedom of the individual comes from the God given strength to live in a hostile world. Prayer to this person becomes meditation. He learns to find within himself the power to live alone. He prays for nothing; he asks for nothing; he may indeed not pray at all. Fortunate is he if he has someone to walk with him. But in the end he will die alone, by himself; no one can take his place in this venture. Should he wish to find in the church of his choice the symbols of history which render themes from the past of Jesus' death and resurrection, all well and good! If not, his freedom cuts him loose to be at-one in the universe, loved and accepted. Now I think God is happy.

To return to "The Marble Faun", Hilda searches through the vast amount of artifacts outside the confessional booths until she perceives her Mother's voice calling her. It is distinct and clear. How appropriate to return once more to hear the Tanager sing. At that moment she dashes into the confessional to pour out her heart to the Priest. No wonder the Priest fulfills his function that day. It is not the church or the Priest, but the place Hilda finds strength in her aloneness. All of us need that. In trying times it is good to have an ally who won't judge or criticize you. In spite of your lack of spiritual depth or in spite of your misdeeds, they still love you. If not, then you need some trysting place to hammer things out. Blood, Sweat and Tears have a song out that speaks to me in gut-wrenching times. "Spinning Wheel" goes like this:

> "What goes up must come down,
> Spinning Wheel got to go round;
> Talking about your troubles, it's a crying sin,
> Ride a painted pony let the Spinning Wheel spin.
> You got no money, you got no home.
> Spinning Wheel all alone,
> Talking about your troubles and you, you never learn,
> Ride a painted pony let the Spinning Wheel turn.
> Did you find a directing sign on the straight and narrow highway?
> Would you like a reflection sign, just let it shine within your mind,
> And show you the colors that are real?
> Someone is waiting just for you,
> Spinning Wheel, spinning true,
> Drop all your troubles by the river side,
> Catch a painted pony on the Spinning Wheel ride!"

Parents need to give their children a right of passage, a right of independence. It is one thing to love your parents; it is quite another to be held accountable to them all of one's life. Parents don't understand the fear and the trepidation the children have, so how can they teach them to cope? It is no wonder we traverse land and sea alone and afraid only to fall into the trap of marrying our mother or father; or worse, we fall into the clutches of someone who promises to lead us to the land of milk and honey, only to control and dominate us as long as we don't know any better.

The next temptation of Jesus comes from the Devil in terms of significance. He takes Jesus to a high mountain to show him all the territory allotted to him which Jesus can call his own if he were to bow to the Devil to worship him. Jesus refuses. In the same manner we too, coming out of the garden, have a deep desire for significance. We yearn for our mother's breast. When things happen to us in the formative stages of our lives, mother is there for us. The minute we find ourselves struggling for freedom, we realize we need to have an alternative plan. We don't want 'Mother' shopping with us, taking us to school or ever hug and kiss us in front of our peers. After maturity, we wonder why we ever did think that way.

In high school if you were lucky enough to play sports, you found a balm for your insecurities. On the other hand, if you were pretty, your significance came through popularity. Many laughed at the band members; today they have their music to play to enthrall others or just simply to meditate by themselves while doing something soothing. There was another kind of person, the smart ones. Yes, some of them were nerdy, but they knew what they wanted and they studied to get it. Those who fell in between spent the years making jokes, trying the teachers patience, living lack luster lives, often in alcohol, because no one recognized their cry for help. They certainly didn't. After school days, we were put out to find new ways to meet an undefined need in our lives. Here sports, unless you were exceptional, and popularity waned. We needed more, but what?

Some find it in their careers. Once we fulfill our desires with something tangible like a title or position, what happens when we lose the position through illness, retirement or worse, neglect? Where has our blanket gone; what is left? Do we curse God and die?

A doctor was asked once who was he when he was not a doctor? He replied, "By God, I am always a Doctor!" Case in point! Woe be unto us if all we have significance in name only.

There seems to me we all have a desire for greatness or self satisfaction. Rather than free us to the world around us, we find we become enslaved by them; the worst possible thing is we don't know it. We have both submission to overt powers, jobs, sports, politics, ideologies and religion and to innate powers like loyalty to family, conscience, inner drives(ego) and what someone else thinks of us. We try to please many of these things in some way or other in order to find significance. It is time we realized that significance comes from within, not in money, prestige or status.

When I grew up, I had no idea of my inner needs. They were met daily in my mystical garden. When I left there, I began to desire for things to replace the lost security I felt. Only I didn't know it then, I found something within me to make me feel a cut above my peers in the towns where we would live for the next six years. I studied hard and I was rewarded by good grades and prestige. In Sunset Park School, in Wilmington North

Carolina, I led the class in handwriting, knowledge, mental games, and I had the leading roles in every play cast for the two years I lived in North Carolina. Roman Gabriel had just begun his road to a successful career in football. He had his significance in sports; I had mine in another way. When the family left there, we went back to Jonesboro, Louisiana, where I had no bargaining power. I wanted to live out my life in Jonesboro, for I felt secure there, but it crippled me because I didn't placate my higher self.

Years later, after a stint in the Marines, one of my friends said he would try to help me get a job at the mill. He told me I was more of the blue collar type than the white collar (where the money was made). I set out from that moment on to prove him wrong. There is nothing wrong with aspiring to do better if you can, but if I had known, I could have been content if only I had self-sufficiency enough to handle my fear of how others would regard me.

In 1969, I had become one of the top managers for a nationwide company; yet, I felt like I did not have all the equipment in my soul for the recognition I needed. Soon after this, I began to have fancy dreams in the night to "answer the call to preach." I just knew God had whispered in my 'ear'. I uprooted my family, two small boys and a wife, and off we went to New Orleans Seminary to equip myself for the ministry. It would take years before I really knew the dynamics behind my 'calling.'

In truth, I think every preacher has the same problem. Whatever the call, they can say, "Yes, it is true, I had a deep need. So what? God can use that as well to help me to understand myself." Once we come to this, we can move on with our lives in truth through the path we choose or to pursue another outside the church.

As for me I had a lesson or two to learn before I came to the hour of decision. In 1976, I went to a small church in north Louisiana. Those people taught me life has significance in small things. However, I wanted more. I sought a position and recognition; and I aspired to be the best known preacher in our state. Because of this I left the best opportunity, (i.e. church and position), anywhere in the world the following year. I would learn much the next seven years; mostly my own stink had corrupted my little garden.

I had a chance to speak to the staff of The Louisiana Baptist Convention after I had learned a few things about myself. The secretary of the department who asked me to speak fretted after he had done so because he thought I might denigrate them in my new found power through this privilege. He would tell me later thanks; then he told of his worry. I didn't disappoint him. My theme was on significance. I told them that it does not come in the title they hold. Many preachers in the convention were envious of them because they secretly wanted to be important and they felt as if the leaders of the convention had reached the pinnacle of 'spirituality.' If they railed against the team, it was because they lacked the ability to get ahead or they had no significance of their own in their calling. I continued on from there to say the significances of our calling lay in a commitment to God; then we should play out our "poem" (our calling) through our chosen vocation, the pastorate or the head of a department in the convention. The calling and our vocation were not equal. I suggested they go to the small churches to bring a little humanity to their program. Make themselves known to the little man and he would have his ego stroked enough perhaps to improve relationships within our denomination.

Every person has a calling from God. We have to try to figure out how we will work out our own salvation in fear and trembling. The small job, the large job, might give significance, but unless you feel good about yourself, you will always fall short. To know yourself will bring happiness; it will end strife; it will cause you to not have to worry about keeping up with the Joneses. If your brother makes more money than you, ask him for a loan. Just kidding! You don't need to feel small and unworthy because you don't have as much as he does. If he looks down his long nose at you, HE has a problem, not you.

Tournier tells of a theory of one of his colleagues. When asked to explain what happens in 'transfer,' that is the relationship between patient and doctor, Dr. Plattner described the psychotherapist's patient as a 'psychotherapeutic agent,' then a 'partner,' and finally as one 'called.' Both the doctor and patient are called by God. It is to that end we are called ("The Naming of Persons").

At this point, I would like to recreate the story of Cain. What if God had met Cain on the day of murder to say to Cain, "So you done gone and done it?" To which Cain replies, "Yeah I did." God then says, "Cain, my son, because of your inner lack of security, you allowed your jealousy to disrupt the fellowship of your family. You have created a situation for yourself where you will roam the world (freedom, but no inner freedom) over to try to find out why you did what you did. You will not have your family's support; others will try to kill you to avenge Abel's death. Therefore I will put a mark on you to protect you which you will carry all your life, unless you find out the meaning of your insignificance. Sin on your part has caused hardships for everyone concerned, not just you. Now I do tell you this: you can use this moment to better your life, or you can live with it always. This sin will enable you to do better; or it will cripple you as you live out your life in continual jealousy and lack of self-esteem."

Cain pulls out, sadden over his confrontation with God. He wanders around until one day he realizes what God had said. His sin comes from his inner insecurity. He is loved. He knows now his sacrifice was accepted; he just sized up the situation wrongly. He establishes an altar in God's name, the God of his ancestors. He preaches salvation through recognizing one's sins to use them as a positive means instead of seeing them as vile and vicious. He preaches everyone has evil, only different in nature, but God has allowed this so he might lift us all to holiness through dealing with our sin (Romans 11:32). Cain becomes king of the land, only in a given year the priest of the church have to come for him to kill him so that he might die to ensure the welfare of his tribe. When the appointed time arrives, the priests kill Cain (without guilt) to fulfill their duty; they bury him in a vineyard where their grapes and wheat are planted. The following year, they reap the first fruits to offer wine and bread to the people in celebration of their lives on behalf of the sacrifice Cain had made. Oh yes, when they buried him, the mark had been lifted.

From Greek mythology we learn of Orestes and Electra. When Agamemnon, their father, comes home from the Trojan War, his wife has taken up with another man. His wife and her lover conspire to kill Agamemnon. The next of kin, which was Orestes, has to avenge the death. In the story, Electra makes sure he does the deed. Electra represents the counter part of Oedipus. She loves her father and wants Orestes to kill their mother. At any rate, Orestes finally does the deed. Because a son or daughter has to respect their parents, he is immediately beset by the furies, or harpies who nag at him continually. One of the goddesses sees his plight; she appeals his case to the tribunal. They feel he is justified and they are ready to set him free when he proclaims, "No. I am guilty. I did it and no other." At that moment, the furies disappeared. He is then purified with the blood of swine (See Gaylen).

In one of my churches, I met a gentleman for whom I had a great deal of admiration. He had been a deacon in our church at one time, but for some reason or other, he had quit coming to church. I visited him to invite him to come to our deacon's supper. He told me he could not because he had been putting his children through college and he had no money to give to the church. He loved the Lord, but he had failed him because he had to quit contributing to the church where they expected 10 % or more. He cried big tears because of his sorrow. He had separated himself from some of the best people on this earth, who would not have held it against him (How about them apples); in fact they would have told him the same thing if he weren't so insecure about his dilemma. As far as I know, he still carries the mark, for he never came back to church. It would require a renunciation of his upbringing to rid him of the mark. He couldn't do it.

If we can't fulfill the obligation to which we have accepted responsibility, we have to have inner fortitude to say, "I no longer can do what I promised; therefore I will resign or I will continue on as long as you understand why." The main thing here is to know if you believe the church is where you need to band your hat, you find a way to coexist. If the church no longer meets your needs, find another or get out; it is okay. Do not hang your head in sorrow and shame. Examine your soul to find out what is right. Don't take prune juice when its wine you need; you learn to find the truth for yourself. The same concept goes for divorce, racial marriages and etc. Of course it helps to have mature people in the church or in your social group to understand. How unfortunate it is for the church to excommunicate an individual who has 'fallen' because of matters of his own doing or beyond his control; or, he is different.

Sometime during the late 1940s Papa dug a pond. Of course Momma wanted geese to swim gracefully on the pond. She ordered the eggs to put in her incubator to hatch herself; then she put them in the pond after they hatched. They were a family. One night an animal, probably a dog, tore all the tail feathers off one poor gander's tail. He lived, but only to remain far behind the herd. I watched for months, the geese foraging for food with him twenty yards or more away. They rejected him until the day he died or he was killed wandering around by himself. When Momma fed them, he had to wait outside the group while they ate. Nothing she could do would ever help the unfortunate goose.

I have the book, "Parzifal", in my library translated by Helen M. Mustard and Charles E. Passage. The author tells the story of Parzifal's desire to become a Knight of the Round Table. Knights, in the days of King Arthur, live to rescue damsels and to seek the Holy Grail. Parzifal's mother has other dreams for him. She does let him go, but dresses him in fool's clothing with an old nag to ride, thinking he would return anon. He succeeds, however, in spite of her clever ruse. On his journey he meets an old, grey headed prince named Gurnemanz. The old Prince teaches him many things like: never ask too many questions; to be thrifty, but generous; show compassion to the needy; to love with all his heart and never to lose his sense of shame. Parenthetically, shame would help him to learn of himself to make corrections or abandon erroneous childhood concept.

On his departure, he meets an old fisherman who tells him of a castle nearby where he might spend the night. Upon Parzifal's arrival at the castle, he is treated fairly in all concerns. There too, he sees the Holy Grail for the very first time. There lives in the castle, it turns out, King Anfortas, who had been made king not by his wishes; but he had a wound which made him impotent. Because his mentor had told him not to ask any questions, he did not ask the King's malady. On the morrow he departed, only to meet his mother's sister's child. She asked him if he had seen the king and if he asked how he came about his injury. He had been told not to ask too many questions so he did not. Sigune then told him in order for the king to be made well an innocent knight must have compassion on the king. The problem is he cannot go back; he has lost the opportunity. From that day forward he resolves to find the king to resolve his wound. Fortunately he later finds the king to heal him.

The wound is the mark. It leaves us impotent; it means we are non-seminal, a dis-incarnation of sorts. I tell people who are different, "You don't have to carry the wound; you are who you are; don't let others tell you that you are bad or what you must think or what you should believe. You face the world bravely because you are loved by God even if the world despises you or seeks to crucify you. Most of all I love you; yet this does not excuse you from transcending other sorrowful traits you may have. Just because you are a minority, gay, religious oriented or not, with freedom comes responsibility. Wear your freedom proudly, yet look deeper, there remains some work to do to attain your goal." Our job as humans is to help those who are wounded.

I wrote this poem for my boys on one occasion:

The Undefeated

I'm thinking of you today,
As you go along your way,
Each with a tremendous test,
A large hindrance in your quest.
Just a step, but none the lest,
Please, always give it your best;
You may lose and you may fail,
But keep the wind in your sail,
For to do so is the why,
That, one day, you'll reach the sky;
And in trials that make you sad,
Know the love of mom and dad.
Oft trials will be repeated,
How so, ne'er be defeated!

The last temptation in the desert requires Jesus to make a spectacle of himself. Jesus says that he will not tempt the Lord in any fashion. How many didos have we pulled in our lives to draw attention to ourselves? While security and significance are important, the need to love and to be loved I feel rates the highest. Marriages often come about because of a deep need for someone to love you. I know that there are other things like sex and money that bring about nuptial endeavors, yet even they don't cover the deepest need of the soul.

We don't know who we are first of all. Since conception, we have many parts. We have our great grandmother's eyes, our grandfather's sexual drive, our grandmother's fear, our dad's asinine ways, our mother's overprotective concerns and our innate, God only knows how far back they go, yearnings. Is it any wonder we are confused and lonely. Then we have the lasciviousness of the raging wolf, the slyness of a fox, the shyness of a turtle, the desire to devour like a hawk, the coo of a dove, the fight of a raging bull, the slipperiness of an eel and finally the consternation of an ass.

In my own family I had Scrooge Mc Duck, Daisy Duck, Hagar the Horrible and Helga, the Pink Panther, Garfield and Odie on one side to influence me. While on the other side I inherited traits from Popeye, Mickey and Minnie Mouse, Luan, Felix and Oscar along with Aunt Bea and Boxcar Willie. My grandfather on my dad's side had faun like characteristics; I loved him to pieces, to borrow a phrase from a cartoon character. I asked my aunt not to tell me her secret, but she did; I had rather not known. Grandmother Clay, a sweet gentle soul with her daughter's secret locked inside, learned to cope with grandpa's antics the only way she knew how; she feigned sickness to have the family to wait on her, mostly Grandpa.

Everyone is legion inside. A part of our ancestors reside in us. We become a fascist if we search for power or a cannibal seeking to eat the other person before he eats us; we are an adulterer if we use the other person we love mostly to our own ends. We don't know who we are; therefore how can we sift through the bile in the jungle of our own excretion. Our minds hold every moment of our lives like a computer; it contains everything we ever knew, but it comes to us in bits and pieces like a gigantic jig saw puzzle. We can't remember if the stories of our past are fact or fiction. We don't remember if an event happened or if we saw a picture of it. We also have a hand-me-down religion that won't hold water in the face of despair. Our bucket leaks at the slightest turmoil; and our volcano erupts at any given moment. Unless we sort through all the rubble, we may never know who we really are.

In Italy, 1858, the time of Hawthorne's sojourn there, a police posse pulled up to a Jewish home to snatch a Jewish child out of a distressed Father's hands. Their cries went around the world. Other Jewish children were kidnapped around this time, but this one had a twist to it. The Catholic serving girl of the family baptized the young boy when he became ill at an early age. She, fearful he might die and not see Heaven, did the deed unknown to the family. The Catholic Church, the ruling power in Italy at that time, when they learned of the incident, took the child to rear him in a special monastery to make sure he became a good Catholic. The justification for the kidnapping: no Christian child could be raised by Jewish parents. This story went around the world; and it would lead to the end of Papal control in Italy, mainly because of little Edgardo Mortara (This entire story is available on the internet).

When the Romans went to church in 1858, all they heard were platitudes or worse, confessionals or self aggradations, but only a cover up to deeper problems. The things they preached against came from the things they detested in their soul, only they had a standard to which they gave rigid attention, offering consolation. A priest could meet these expectations so he need not try to find out who he was or he just might crumble. Yet they sought to convert the heretic, the Protestants. The cry on the street became, "What church can disinfect my soul?"

In the hospital where I serve as part-time chaplain, the priest holds a service called "The Anointing of the Hands." Each participant from the staff, regardless of status or position, comes to offer their hands for the anointing of the oil. They present their hands to symbolize their commitment to ministry. As the ministers place the oil on their palms, the ministers recite a prayer of dedication. It comes close to the donning of the apron by Jesus, a worldwide symbol of ministry to which the church is called. Then all join in unison and repeat the following:

> Nurses Hands
> Blessed be these hands that have touched life.
> Blessed be these hands that have felt pain.
> Blessed be these hands that have embraced with compassion.
> Blessed be these hands that have been clinched in anger or withdrawn in fear.
> Blessed be these hands that have drawn blood and administered medicine.
> Blessed be these hands that have cleaned beds and

disposed of wastes.
Blessed be these hands that have anointed the sick and
offered blessings.
Blessed be these hands that grow stiff with age.
Blessed be these hands that have comforted the dying and
held the dead.
Blessed be these hands: we hold the future in these
hands.
Blessed be our hands for they are the work of your hands,
O Holy One.

(This Blessing of the Hands is from "In Praise of Hands" Diann Neu, Waterwheel, Winter 1998). When the leaders of the church forget this truth, their adherents become robots with oil cans to grease the wheels of the institution!

Desert Storm

Behold the eye,
While outward, monsters,
Breathe fire, inward!
Collective faith,
No still, small voice.
Bishops echo, satanic words!
The cold, cruel master,
Denies individualism,
Dogma defined,
Pavlov's dog created!
Carved blocks,
Move as robots,
Remote control,
Ready to die for "salvation?"
Insights darkened,
While outward, lightning blasts,
Fill the night,
To bring freedom, inward!

And the Protestant churches of the sixties and seventies weren't much better than the scene presented in the Hawthorne era. Try reading this poem to see if you agree:

The Sixties

The fifties in Louisiana were euphoric for us,
In order to get to school, we all had to ride a bus,
LSU had become the national champs,
The post office still sold three cents stamps;
However, February 3, 1959, should have been a portent,
That we had entered the summer of our discontent,
For this was the infamous day the music died;
Then when Robert, Martin and John fell, we cried.
For the very first time Richard would marry Liz,
The mustang and the see-through blouse were a whiz,
LBJ would smoke Goldwater and blaze the war in Nam,
And later Nixon would hold America in his palm.
Words from "Louie, Louie" caused in Indiana outrage,
While Beatle mania was the current craze,
Words like 'conscientious objectors' came to fore,
Joan Baez, Jane Fonda and others all said "No more!"
We had sit-ins and violence over the war and race,
The old home town was not the same place.
The church was silent and many youth left the pew,
There were hippies, yuppies and the SDS with a view,
They went to Kent State, formed ultra religious groups,
Jeered the USA by burning flags and hating our troops,
Wore wrinkled clothes, hair oddly styled,
Frustrated parents were certainly riled.
Signs like 'Make love, not war,' and 'Flower Power,'
Signaled the end of the Arthur Godfrey hour.
Solutions? Answers? All said 'Be damned if I know!'
A different drummer still boomed from Fats Domino;
The Supremes led the Mo Town set,
And from Elvis, nothing but net!
Ray Charles gave us the beat and the thrill;
We went 'Walking to New Orleans' and found 'Blueberry Hill;'
The story of the land of liberty the poet's tol',
Through the medium of that ole time Rock and Roll!!!

Into this world I came, totally unaware, to marry another with no idea
of whom I was behind the mask; then I became a preacher of the gospel.
The mask was me, not my self, strutting like a cat on a hot tin roof. Finding
solace in another to give me her breast, and a congregation that would

love me until the cows came home seemed to be the answer. Hello? Try going into these two events as a Dr. Jekyll and Mr. Hyde facing neurotic tendencies in your partners. My bucket would eventually get a bigger hole in it because I had to courtesy before the congregation as they called the dance. The music was not my style, but my calling made it obligatory. Besides where can a man go without a job; another church would be afraid to chance your demand for freedom. Therefore you are once again alone in a hostile world. Then as the more you begin to question the 'bun' thinking, your wife doesn't understand you. "Why can't you just accept things just as the Bible says?" In other words, "Get back in that Bible."

My time on the stage had only just begun, for I felt as if I were always striving to please someone, including my parents. The coup de gras, I allowed others to dump their piles on me without a word, all in the name of Jesus or maybe low self-esteem. Act Two ended in 1984 in divorce from both wife and church.

Why could I not have said, "Hey this is me?" But no, I have to act in all kinds of unjustified behavior, to be a jerk who doesn't know himself nor love himself. And I haven't gotten much better yet. Sometimes in the heat of the blood I still let it all hang out. But life goes on. As Sinatra croons:

> That's life, that's what all the people say,
> You're riding high in April, shot down in May,
> But I know I'm gonna change that tune,
> When I'm back on top in June.

> I've been a puppet, a pauper, a pirate, a poet, a pawn and a king,
> I've been up and down and over and out,
> And I know one thing, each time I find myself flat on my face,
> I pick myself up and get back in the race.

Bultmann said we could not be sure of the Bible stories, so we are confronted in the present by the foolishness of the Gospel. This day is the day of salvation. Our lives are also a myth to which we can make little sense. We are fragmented; yet we can go with this one constant. We can continue to live out our lives in narcissism, thinking we are the center of the world; or we discover what our deepest longing is and we seek to find it. Our deepest need is 'to love and to be loved', heaven if you will. The Pentecostals are right when they say, "We can almost see heaven from here." However they look in the wrong direction. Heaven is within their souls as well as yours and mine. Besides, heaven is not rapture; it's a dance. I certainly don't want to miss the dance.

THE DANCE

See the butterfly flit, from flower to flower;
Watch bees buzz by, seeking honey power,
Then the rabbit sits with his funny little nose itch,
While in a tree nearby lies the squirrel with a tail twitch.
Dogs barking with a shimmy,
Cats purring, as if saying 'A little love gimme!'
Birds searching for a mate, preen,
Peacocks strut, with gowns of blue, red and green,
Snakes twist to show their clout,
Making rodents scurry, shakin' their booty all about;
And I with an accordion can not play,
For fear of what orthodoxy might say!

Think not of what others say, just age,
Grow to maturity to uncage,
Inhibitions, to live with fervor,
As a child of god, a survivor,
To offer this life a lasting gift,
While others through the sands of time sift;
Choreograph a dance into rhyme,
Create this eternal space of time,
A poem of purpose, a reason,
To make your life a waltz each season.

If the reader will allow me to reinterpret the story of the garden, I will now do so. Perhaps it may be a little tiresome since I already restructured the Cain story, but here goes.

Adam and Eve came to the tree of knowledge together. They saw the fruit as a step toward their development. They squeezed the juice from the fruit, allowing it to ferment for a while. Then they partook. They laughed and played for hours. Their frolic was like two merry souls at the Mardi Gras. The serpent even taught them how to do the twist. When God heard the ruckus, he came to inquire. In this story they told him the truth. He replied:

"I see you are now ready to strike out into the world alone. Give me a cup of your wine while I explain a few things. You remember, I told you not to eat of the tree of good and evil. I knew one day when you were ready you would defy my orders. I protected you from the 'outside' until you reached an age where you could cope in the world out there as a mother bird watches her brood. Here you have had a magical time, with my constant mothering. You do not know the trials ahead of you nor are you prepared for what you will see and hear. Out there the world has yet to be harnessed. Suffering will occur in the toil of the day to make the world a better place to live. Animals await to kill or be killed. Eve will have great pain in child birth, for we have no antiseptic to aid her, and if we did she would still suffer." Adam says, "Lord, what is suffering?" God said, "Suffering is the hardships you will have in the outside world, pain, aloneness and death. Without suffering, however, you will not know the depths of your soul for through suffering your inner self will be honed.

You have been babes here; there you will have to manage as adults. Things you have never known are foreign to you. You can know nothing of pain, anxiety, fear, joy and love if you have not experienced them. I will be a wisp in the world, no longer coming to your every need. I will be there for you, but not so much as you think. You will be an amateur in a cruel world. There you will find yourselves alone; and all you will have is your wits. You will have to invent things necessary to live. Even your image of me will be vague. You will see me in myths, dreams and wonders, but you will have to create words to describe the revelation. They will be varied, but all point to the kernel of truth which I reveal through those mediums. There will be no more face to face encounters.

Houses will have to be built. Children with enormous problems will be born to you. Your memory of this place will grow faint; but you will be in search of this communion all your life. Mark it well, when your sons and daughters leave your garden, they will also have the same needs as you have now. How well you teach them won't matter, because they won't be able to remember all of it anyway. You are ill prepared for the world, but you will have to cope with the means you have. You will make many mistakes, especially in child rearing, because you do not have anyone to tell you how. Even if you did, you will still make errors. Your children in turn will also make many mistakes after they leave home. Show them love the best that you can; when the time comes, as your time has now come, put them out to find their true selves in the valley of sorrow. They will either live out their lives in personal pursuits or they will learn to live and to love and to rekindle the joy they had with you.

Now go with my blessing; but remember this, become as one, for in oneness you will find your ultimate freedom. As for that dance Mr. Snake, you were wonderful, but alas, you must now be put in your place as well. I am sorry, but in the new world you and these people won't get along very well."

Tyros indeed! Aren't we all? Talk about existential! Shakespeare said, "All the world's a stage; all the men and women merely players" ("As you Like It," Act Two; Scene 7). We all just have different scripts; but we all search for the same thing. From "Macbeth" we get the one constant in all our hearts:

> "Two truths are told, as happy prologues to the swelling act of the imperial theme. I thank you, gentlemen. This supernatural soliciting cannot be ill, cannot be good; if ill, why hath it given me earnest of success, commencing in a truth? I am thane of Cawdor; if good, why do I yield to that suggestion whose horrid image doth unfix my hair and make my seated heart knock at ribs against the use of nature? My thought, whose murder yet is but fantastical, shakes so my single state of man that function is smothered in surmise, and nothing is but what is not."

In truth, we all have a deep desire to live, yet within we have something that calls for justice. That is the return to the garden, communion once again with mother. To love and to be love brings us home again. Our job becomes the will to discover what reality really means.

El Nino

Armed, wooden soldiers,
Fell Babylon's house of dreams,
Curious virgin child banned,
From the womb,
The tree of knowledge;
And I am left in his heat,
To parch my trickling wadi.

As day wanes, she sends the night princess,
Who peeks coquettishly behind soft clouds,
While one by one her ensemble,
Awakens to a rhythmic dance,
Breaking my personal drought,
And I am renewed to love again.

Her silvery face obtains a golden glow,
Sending amber waves
To enter blinded portals,
Ricocheting through corridors,
Echoing into chambers of red,
A global warming,
Flushing cobwebs of hand-me-down myths,
Still with the ability to cast ebony shadows
Of her yet unsolved mysteries.

I am now haunted once again,
And thirst for my quest, her path,
Even allow dusty, packed desires,
Hot, silky memories,
To chortle in my soul,
Defying infrequent laughter,
And eagerly await his coming.

Modus Vivendi

The four creation stories give us a clue as to the position, or life styles, many parents often assume. God represents the religious parent, "Thou shalt not." Tiamat offers us an idea of an anal retentive parent; the fat serpent represents an anal attentive mom until she tires of their play. Zeus brings to the table the last type, authoritative. For the fifth position I will use the ole Freudian angle of sex as a lifestyle. Finally, I will try to show us a way out of our dilemma. Even with help, it will still take a lot of practice to achieve our goal.

The child on the other hand will respond in three ways. The responses come from the sense of fright or fight syndrome. The third position is the creative response. As children, we mostly use the first two. 'Obey or else'! 'No way, Mom'! Either way you lose. Tom Sawyer used his creative brain to escape his orders. One day he has to whitewash the fence. He rebelled for a time, and then acquiesced. He didn't like it, but it was the better of two options. However when his friends come by to laugh at him, he cons them into doing his work by pretending he was having "too" much fun.

My wife told me her dad was on the authoritative side. He would tell her no, but her mother had taught her underneath he was really a softy. Consequently, she would run her fingers through his hair to curl it with one of her fingers. Now what man could resist that? Talk about creative. This could lead to manipulation also.

Rebellion is not a bad thing. In the garden, Adam and Eve rebel against God's orders. In essence, it is the first step toward real freedom. The world sees it as sin. When a child rebels, the parents see it as defiance. I don't suggest a child rebel until he gets away on his own. There are a lot of advantages to holding your temper until later, like eating, sleeping and a place to live. For our purposes, let us think of submission and rebellion as the elder brother and the prodigal. The elder brother stays home to dutifully obey his parents. He is the good guy. The prodigal has always been a handful with a zestful, inquisitive nature. He may well indeed cause a stir before long, especially with strong willed, opinionated parents.

Submission may not necessarily be a bad thing either. Sometimes men and women alike submit to have a spirit of cooperation. If a man agrees to do the dishes, his friends say he is hen pecked. If he elects to be with his wife rather than go out on the town, he really gets hoorayed. The wife hurries home to cook rather than stop off for cocktails with the girls and they cast dispersion on her as well. The truth of the matter, both have a deeper commitment than any of their friends. Actually, the friends secretly want the same thing.

I realize I am drawing a fine line between attentive and retentive. Attentive means courtesy and devotion. Retentive means good memory recall or being able to retain. The best example of these comes from the movie "The Odd Couple". Oscar and Felix give us an example of each. Felix freaks out over the least thing being out of a set order. Oscar, on the other hand, could care less if things are in disarray. Thus a constant battle ensues. Felix must have been easy to potty train, while Oscar held his back. One day Felix rebels. He leaves a note saying he was leaving and he signed it simply F. U. I am sure a lot of times when we get fed up, we may think the thought delivered, but it actually means Felix Unger.

Somewhere in the early years (during the magical kingdom) the child puts on the mask of one or more of these parental types. He will assume the role of acceptance or of rejection of his parent's altogether; or he may accept one parent and not the other. When he becomes an adult, unless he recognizes his stance, he will act out his role in everyday life until he transcends his initial upbringing.

The following types are used to show the level or plane on which some live out their lifestyles. If I use a man or woman, it is because it is in the story I am telling. I do not mean them to say women are like this; or that men are like that. The gender is coincidental.

First, let me use the anal retentive type to illustrate the hypothesis. Today, 12-27-1903, I heard a story about a Norwegian man who showed up for his drivers test drunk. He started taking an additional test to get his license to drive a big rig when the attendant realized he reeked of liquor. The employee called the police and they of course arrested him. They seized his vehicle which he had driven over an hour to take his test. He had to take the bus home with a DUI to boot. Now that was a jerk.

Jeff Foxworthy has made a living telling 'redneck' jokes. We get a kick out of them; in reality, there probably lies a great deal of truth in them. If one wants to be a 'redneck,' so be it. Take the following for example:

I'm a Redneck

You can catch me with my pants unzipped,
Taking mayo from a jar, finger dipped,
Chewing tabacky with a drool down the jaw,
Running around the double-wide in the raw.
Can fix anything with my hands,
Using wire or rawhide that expands;
Spit on the floor of the ole barn,
Say a few choice word stronger than darn,
Ride the ole tractor from dawn til dust,
Don't care if the tools begin to rust,
Plant the garden using store bought seeds,
Who cares if nuttin grows but weeds!
Ride in my truck with dents a few,
Hell, they only show that I'm making a haul or two;
Strong as an ox, but likes a rub,
Then relax in my big ole garden tub,
Lay up all night watching TV,
Sleep til the sun is straight over me,
Work just because I like to eat,
To win the lottery would be quite a treat,
Then I'd lounge in my overalls, in my mouth a straw,
Drive my truck to the bank and some money withdraw,
Now everything I do or drive might still be a wreck,
But hey, who cares, for I'm a redneck!

It's okay to be a redneck, just don't carry it too far. Remember what Tennyson said in "Locksley Hall":

"As the husband is, the wife is: Thou art mated with a clown,
And the grossness of his nature will have weight to drag thee down."

The parental model of the retentive type may also include a very permissive nature. They indulge their children to a fault. Perhaps these parents react from a very strict home life. They vow when they are very young (How many vows did we make that will haunt us until we give ourselves the authority to let them go?) that they would not treat their children the way they were reared. The vow here leads them down a very dangerous path.

We had peers in grade school who got more than anyone else; their parents made sure we 'lesser mortals' knew just how much they loved their children in ostentatious ways. More than likely these children will retain the home life of the parents. They in turn will spoil their children. There is nothing wrong in giving to a child, but when it causes him or her to want someone to wait on them all of their lives, lookout.

Next we have the religious type. I received an e-mail two days ago about a woman driver who had pulled up behind a man at a stop light. When the light turned green the man could not go. His car had stalled, but she didn't know why he hadn't moved; so she blew her horn at him; before long she began to curse. When the light turned green again, and he didn't budge, she became livid, turning beet red in the face. A policeman tapped on her window to ask her to get out of the car. He immediately arrested her. When the dust settled at the police station, she asked him why she had been arrested. He said, "Ma'am, I saw the bumper sticker on the back of your car which read: 'Follow Me To Sunday School' and the chrome plated fish emblem on the trunk and the license plate holder saying 'Jesus Loves All of us'. When I saw how you were acting, I thought perhaps you had stolen the car." And she thought the man in front of her was a bustard.

In one of my churches in the seventies, I received a call from a distraught parent. I found out upon my arrival to their home that the daughter had rejected her parent's religious life. She claimed they had no commitment, no deep convictions. She had found a college group that had zing. She told of the pastor getting off a plane, returning from some conference talking to thousands of adherents. He asked, "Where is your commitment? You still have television in your home. You still are tied to 'things'." That afternoon the church members had a big bond fire; there they burned all those 'things' including the TVs. She did join that church. The last I heard of her, she still belonged to the church, but it had settled into a normal, routine. In other words, she had returned to the same level of commitment as her forefathers. She rebelled against nominal Christianity to quietly accept a more dominate form of control, only to end up accepting the 'bun' life.

There is nothing wrong with maintaining the same type of church membership that the parents had. The problem lies in never questioning the beliefs of your chosen church. To accept everything as absolute is to fall into the trap of having others tell you what to believe. There won't be any autonomous thinking, just living in the 'bun.' I have a friend who never goes to church. When asked about her church affiliation, she says the name of the denomination to which her mother attended. She doesn't know one thing about the church, but it must be the 'true' church because her mother belonged.

The third position one takes is anal attentive. I overheard one man say that when he goes to the bathroom in the middle of the night his wife arises to remake the bed. I know he is kidding. It is one thing to like a clean house, but if after it is clean you can't use the commode for six hours, what do you do; go off the front porch? I wrote this poem to illustrate how we can become a little obsessive in our anal attentive ways:

The Crumb

It was just before dawn; Bubba found himself alone,
Nobody but him and the telephone;
So he decided to write a poem of effort,
Of a crumb he dropped, a certain ort.
"Who hid it from me," he thought as he searched in vain?
He knew it would be found by another to his loss of gain;
But hey, he had plenty of time,
To find the speck, to avoid being labeled slime.
Find it he cannot at a quarter after three,
And he doesn't look forward to her coming with glee,
Still he searched on his knees,
Afraid to make another mess, not even sneeze,
Fruitless it seems, his mind now in despair,
The damage is done, beyond repair,
The dread hour arrives with a kindly bustle,
And off to the computer room he did hustle;
His fears, not unfounded, soon came unsought,
Against whom the whole day he had fought,
Through the medium of that mournful sound,
"What's this on the floor I've found?"

Men can be anal about their toys too. I know a carpenter that I use from time to time. He is a very good carpenter. He has not come up to par in the world with all the power tools available because he just likes to use his old equipment. One day he tells me about a barn he contracted to build. It seems the old 'gentleman' who pays the bill had a shop full of 21st century power tools. Everyday he made fun of the worker and his tools. Not only that, but he scrutinizes every inch of the handyman's work. Naturally, he would not find satisfaction in the builder's work. It lacked perfection because he didn't use good tools. No need for me to ask if he offers to lend the old saw horse any of his 'stuff.' He does not. I didn't ask, but I should have, "Why didn't the owner build it himself?"

The fourth type of personality comes from the authoritarian mode. There are many parents who are totalitarian in their homes; some even take it to work with them. In sales, we learn the various types of managers in order to get the sale. Each of the four types is represented in managerial strategies. In the home in this fourth role, a woman will submit to a domineering man because she submitted to her parents. She was punished if she did badly. Therefore she allows him to dominate her now. A male will take a woman's abuse also because he had been taught to 'be seen and not heard.' When one gets the courage to stand up to the abusive one, divorce becomes a reality without both finding out about their vicious drive to dominate and to submit. It won't do much good to clean up the 'act' unless they strive to redeem their souls. This rebirth requires more than a few hot tears. It takes atonement to which we shall return shortly.

A person can also be driven to control in subtle ways. Mostly this type speaks in 'imperatives.' Sometimes the driven person does not realize the action. A man will get a drink of water. Before he puts the glass down, his wife tells him where to put it. One lady said to her husband on the way to the kitchen to put the glass in its place, "When you get through with that glass put it down in the sink." Where was he going to put it, back in the cabinet? While a wife is brushing her teeth, the husband will say, "Be sure you put the top back on the toothpaste and put it back where you found it." Where was she going to put it, in the shower? Now if you are an anal retentive person, you probably need someone to tell you to clean up your mess. However, if you are the opposite, you get about thirty of these directives in a day and you are ready to take a "slow boat to China."

I am sure you have met the person who knows everything. They are arrogant and self-opinionated. Perhaps you have seen the commercial of the four guys in a car taking a trip. The driver talks incessantly. The other three can't hear because they have their radio's speakers plugged into their ears. One guy's batteries run out and he almost faints because the driver still gives a running narrative as he drives. The next one's batteries run out and he lays his head back on the seat in utter frustration and nausea. Meanwhile the fourth continues to listen to his radio because he has long-lasting batteries. Need I say more?

Ever since 9:11 I have wondered why a person would submit themselves to a dictator like Saddam or Osama. Can they not see the destructive nature of the power-hungry mongrels? Is it because they find a certain amount of freedom in their acceptance?

Or is it because they fear reprisal to themselves or to their families. Perhaps it comes from a little of both. Some readily submit for fear of slavery, chaos or slaughter. Many of the Arabs hate the liberators (especially the USA) so they rather keep what they have than to allow democracy.

As far as dictators go, none of them throughout the years have been anything but evil. They represent wickedness incarnate. Yet they all think the best of themselves. Order abounds. If any one disagrees with the dictator's methods, they keep it to themselves or face the consequences. Can't you just hear Saddam saying to the insurrectionist now, "Look what a mess the Americans have made in our country. My, my!"

And what about the suicide bombers? Their religion tells them the ultimate sacrifice comes from killing one's self to destroy his enemy represents the highest good; a warrior such as this can expect many great rewards in the hereafter. It seems I have heard something similar to this before, like rubies and palaces; dare I mention, 'you shall reap great rewards on earth for allowing God to be your partner.'

Did not many slaves stay on the plantation because of fear of the unknown? Remember, the bailiwick where they lived represented the only world they knew, especially the ones born on the place. Many stayed because they had been treated fairly or shall we say, brain washed to the point they knew no better.

It doesn't take a 'rocket scientist' to figure out that if a person marries a strong willed personality and he or she is the opposite, the 'fur will fly.' Depending on whether one submits or rebels will determine his approach. The authoritarian person won't change unless he or she gets redirected.

Sometimes they marry someone just like mom or dad. Therefore they will repeat the same action as when they were small. Most arguments will occur when these roles are played out. They will never stop until the couple realizes from where they come. It is not nagging; it is the why of the nagging. Is it because of an anal retentive male; or is it because of an overbearing wife?

Rather than fight, try, in Joan Rivers words, to say, "Can we talk?" Where is the creative side in all of this? Somewhere along the way, we have had our creative side beaten out of us; or we have been taught to use the left side of our brains only. Let me demonstrate. In my first marriage, my mother in law told me that my children had too much spirit. She said I had to break their spirit to make them behave. In other words, we had to keep them from creative responses. Now to be sure, they have to learn to obey the rules, we can do that without breaking them like a horse.

In my grammar school years, I had one principle and one teacher who sought to bring out the creativity in me. John Haile and Mrs. Willingham gave me the most encouragement. In 1953, my parents lived in Wilmington, North Carolina. As I have stated previously, I attended Sunset Park School. That school had every teacher in it on the lookout for creative ways to enrich the right side of our brains. We had art classes, drama classes, a band and a glee club which we could attend.

So what, other schools do also? The point is that each teacher in each class didn't just teach by lecture; they used spelling, geography and math bees. The students worked in teams to compete against the other side. Believe me it worked; we studied because we did not want to lose. I had more creativity there than any other time in my life. After two years, we moved back to Jonesboro where Mrs. Shively was the only teacher in high school who tried to get me to go higher; my French teacher in college did her best to get me to use my talents; no one, not even in seminary, ever tried again.

Every time you are in contact with another person represents an existential moment. You will get along very well unless confronted with your demons. If penned down, you will submit or react to your need to submit. Why not train yourself to creativity in these encounters? The subjective mood will play itself out in your life unless you learn to be objective enough to say, "Hey I have a problem. I need you to help me work it out." Perhaps your reaction might just well enough be to submit to avoid a fight. But you make that decision to do so in an adult manner. Later, when the blood cools, you can discuss the issue.

Back to the elder and his little brother, the one doing the submission will have the hardest row to hoe. He will not need to change nor will he feel he has sinned. Hence he becomes free to judge and to follow simple rules to seal his admission in heaven, the ultimate goal. In the class with the study of "Forty Days of Purpose" the author asks the class to divide up to discuss some pertinent questions. My group had the question, "How would knowing God's purposes help you focus your life?" Answers come in terms of hope, peace, motivation and the ultimate, victory over death (i.e. heaven). My answer reaches across the spectrum of each existential moment. It requires us to be patient when the person in front of us doesn't go immediately when the light turns green or a waitress doesn't bring our food as fast as we want her to do it. My answer puts the onus on us to understand others, accept others as a person of worth and value and building relationships with all, not the ones we can pick or choose in each moment we have. One of the members says, "Yeah, I can see this. I have my mind on the big picture, but he brings it to every day living." Where else is it? The elder type often seems saved and satisfied. They miss the mark; Bonhoeffer calls this cheap grace.

Perhaps we should ask ourselves just who the elder brothers really are. They sit in the pew; they have their knees on the prayer rail; they hold the positions of service in the church and I am in the middle of them. Until we see ourselves as the elder, we will never reach our full potential as a true human being. As long as the preacher rails against the vile, vicious degradations of the prodigals, we shout 'Amen!' When he gets to messing around in our hen house, we take him to task. I don't know why it is, but if someone confronts us with the truth, we feel we have to kill them. What we have in the church today is more 'spiritual intoxication' than humility. Some where down the line we have to quit our 'elderberry' ways!

The elder brother hides in the church; he develops a good rapport with all by being a Holy Joe; he attacks evil in every conceivable corner. With the inability to love coupled with his hunger for recognition comes his jaundiced vision of the evil in the prodigal, while exonerating himself through his commitment. One can't help but wonder what happens when he is elected to a high position in the church, a wine keg with no air hole. Then he marries a woman who will put up with him because the Bible says she has to do so. She waits on him; she puts up with his whining. Hopefully someone will come along one day to shoot her to end the misery.

Robert Burns sat in church one time. A lady sat in the pew in front of him with a fruit basket looking hat on her head. As he observed, a louse raised its ugly head on her hat. He wrote:

"O wad some gift the giftie gie us to see ourselves as others see us!"

To return to Jessie James once more, we all have our two selves. In order for the true self to come into play, we will need a 'rebirth' from the package of imprints bestowed upon us. As I have shown, they can be either innate or acquired through the early years of our lives. They determine our thoughts, politics and religious preferences. Some we will keep; some we need to examine to see if they are excess baggage; or if at least, they need honing. We have them; it is not our fault. However, if we don't know what they do to us, how can we change? I do volunteer work at one of the hospitals in Alexandria, La. My station resides in the outpatient blood lab. There the workers draw blood; they have a name for this, Phlebotomist. Just because I can spell the term and I have the hours in the 'gym' doesn't mean that I can draw blood. I try to lend my services and no patient accepts my offer. Will you?

It will take more than putting on a suit and tie to overcome the demons in our soul. I wrote a poem once about how no matter hard we try we still have some of our old habits hanging around which we have to conquer.

The poem shows how we can quit acting in some ways, but unless there is a commitment to excellence every day, we may end up showing our derrieres quite often. It also shows our imperfection which laughs at one's own self. If this be true of us, why can't we tolerate the speck in our brother's eye? Besides, we all know the ending of fairy tales, "and they lived happily ever after." In our own lives at least we know that is a crock. However, if we incorporate a little right brain (feminine) thinking into our left brained heads, we might just find an answer to our quest.

In this poem, Bud makes a change; does he change by putting on a new suit, or does he really make a creative change? If the former, his anal retentiveness will surely come into conflict with her anal attentiveness! If the latter, they have a chance to build a beautiful life only if they both control their excessive behavior. If she doesn't change, sooner or later Bud's old self will emerge, perhaps with vengeance.

On Becoming a Prince

In a land far, far away,
On prince's pond some say,
Lived a frog named Bud Weiser,
And a beaut named Janis Riser.
Now Bud was crass and coarse,
While J.R. tended her pad,
Helping her folks, dear Mom and Dad.
Ole bud would sit each day flicking flies,
Ne'er moving, on just his long tongue he relied.
One day he noticed this Queen,
So, he licked himself clean and began to preen,
And sauntered up to Miss Janis' side,
To ask, "Will you be my bride?"
"Not on your life you slothful ole toad,
Hit the road Jack, hit the road!"
Off he went but did avow,
This tadpole he would wow.
He cleaned up his act, e'en his belching did retract,
For you see, Bud had become wiser,
And in days to come, would get a little Weiser!

Before we leave this section, one other thought comes to mind. Often a person, not necessarily an elder brother, withholds the submission slip in order to justify his freedom. If he encounters a strong willed individual determined to get control, he will get angry at his desire to submit, perhaps resentful at having submitted to his parents. Then he will fight. He has been pushed to the limit. He actually has no freedom at all, hiding in his cocoon. His freedom comes from his being helpful and kind. His alter ego wishes he were strong enough to whip all the bullies in the world. If he does say no, he feels guilty.

Maturity teaches him when to submit and when to say no. When he says no, he doesn't have to feel guilty. When he says no to a bully, the brat is going to try to conquer him anyway. Unless he remains calm, the fight is on. To find creative ways to say no will require an attained skill he never had before.

The prodigal on the other hand will find relationships marred with his parents because he is recalcitrant. Two types occur. One rebels to find himself; he begins his search. He may very well end up in the gutter of his own making, but he will arise wiser. He may or may not take up his parent's religion. In regards to their behavior, he will adopt a pattern of his own, hopefully more connected to reality. The second type will become anal retentive; he will reject all religion, or remain nominal at best. He will live to himself, feeding his own ego to the detriment of anyone. He is loved only by himself; he uses others to get his way. He sees women as an end in themselves, for his own pleasure. He is most nearly recognized as the citizens of Sodom and Gomorrah who sought to keep others away so that they might enjoy the wealth for themselves, even to the point of abuse. In other words a jerk!

Your subjective self is your experience. Your value system comes from years of being taught, or at least an attempt, to make judgments of right and wrong. The old saying, "Let your conscience be your guide," is erroneous. You can replace some of the archaic vows, thoughts, religion and roles you play by objective perusal. The problem lies when young people think the way they were taught is truth; they therefore do not allow liberal arts schools to challenge their thought patterns. They live in a closed society; they will always live in darkness.

There is a major difference between conceived and preconceived notions. Conceived notions come from the germ, or birth, of an idea. It comes from a creative source within or from some new knowledge made available through education. Preconceived notions remain in your brain because of early training from parents, peers or church. To grow, one must be able to discern whether their preconceived concepts may have merit or not.

In 2003 Louisiana College, a Southern Baptists Liberal Arts facility in Pineville, Louisiana, banned two books from their library. One of the books came from M. Scott Peck, "The Road Less Traveled". The reason: Peck used two or three colorful expletives. Some of the students complained to the president of the school and out the books went. Did they not know that Peck was not a Christian when he wrote the book. Because of the writing, he came to know Jesus? Plus, the book contained more truths than they had ever heard in their cozy nooks back home.

Those students have a rude awakening coming; the real world gets a little more daring than that. When their experience teaches them they held the wrong assumption, they may just have to say like O. J.'s lawyer, "If it doesn't fit, you have to acquit!" My question would be, "Why pay for college; you already know more than the professors and Dr. Peck?" Besides, I'll wager they already speak the language.

For an update on the story, after this manuscript had been completed in some areas, the faculty came to the rescue to have the book reinstated to the library. I know some of these people and I will tell you that they are all super fine, autonomous thinkers.

The next lifestyle refers us to the over zealous attention given to sex. Freud says all our problems stem from our sexual inclinations. Much has been written to refute his theory, however for our purposes at the present we will look at the two types of thought predominate in men and women in regards to a life style of sexual behavior. I am talking about the sexual prowess that drives one's life style, not wholesome sexual behavior that comes from intimacy. Here you will find the Cro-Magnon, male chauvinist, macho type male who thinks about nothing but using a woman for his own end. The woman is reduced to an object rather than a person of worth and value. They do not care for long relationships; however if they get married after the honeymoon is over, there is no depth for a relationship. How many women have married a he-man only to find out later all he had was his joy stick? I have a cute story saved on my computer about some female cells being injected into a male brain. When the girls arrive, they cannot find any males around. They become very disappointed. They start to check out of the upper room when they hear a very distant voice saying, "We are down here!" Sometimes we do need calibration.

Some years back, a very pretty lady with three children told me she had never had a climax. She said her 'ex' husband hopped on to please himself, never thinking about her needs. She felt cheated, hurt and guilty all at the same time. Somehow she blamed herself. The good news, she went on to find happiness and sexual bliss with a person who made her come alive inside.

Don't think men are by themselves in this. A friend of mine told me of an all girl's club to which he belonged. He and his wife were the only married couple in the forum. Each time they met, all the girls would discuss would be sex; and how they hoped to meet one of the men described above that night. The next time they met, if the girls got lucky, all they wanted to do was describe the size of his phallus. Generally they started at a foot or more. If he had a small penis, they did not tell who he was, but they might as well have because they gave his rank and occupation. None of them wanted to marry, so they said, but the first proposal they took him up on it.

Notice I said marry, not love. Perhaps they are incapable of love. One thing for sure, sexual pleasure doesn't mean love. One thing going for these people, at least they are not dysfunctional, not sexually anyway. I believe many marriages and relationships fail not because of the fact their sex lives didn't jive, it is because that was all there was to that. One of Miss Peggy Lee's hits said:

> Is that all there is to love?
> Is that all there is?
> If that's all there is to that,
> Then let's keep dancing,
> Let's break out the booze and have a ball!
> If that's all there is?

The other side of the coin shows frigidity and impotence. Fromm says:

> Love is not the result of adequate sexual satisfaction, but sexual happiness—even the knowledge of the so-called sexual technique—is the result of love. If aside from everyday observation, this thesis needed to be proved, such proof can be found in ample material of psychoanalytic data. The study of the most frequent sexual problems— frigidity in women, and the more or less severe forms of psychic impotence in men—show that the cause does not lie in a lack of knowledge of the right technique, but in the inhibitions which make it impossible to love. Fear of or hatred for the other sex are at the bottom of those difficulties which prevent a person from giving himself completely, from acting spontaneously, from trusting the sexual partner in the immediacy and directness of physical closeness. If a sexually inhibited person can emerge from fear or hate, and hence become capable of loving, his

or her sexual problems are solved. If not, no amount of knowledge about sexual techniques will help" (The Art of Loving pg 75).

Now, just for fun, try putting each of the above lifestyles together in various ways to see what the outcome will be. I already said Bud and Janis Weiser have to conquer their inner selves. Let's pretend they don't. What do you think will happen the first time Bud comes in reeking of stale flies and mud on his legs. What if he wants to eat in the den (that she has just cleaned) rather than the kitchen? You supply the answers. Mix and match the five positions stated above to create a marriage with each type. It should be fun. After you do it, try to picture your own marriage or a relationship you are in. What do you see? Remember we are what we see.

"Pussy Cat, Pussy Cat, where you been?
Been around the world and I am going again.
Pussy Cat, Pussy Cat, where have you been?
Been to London to see the Queen.
Pussy Cat, Pussy Cat, what did you see there?
I saw the mouse under her chair!"

The reason you should do this is two-fold. One, it will help you to see yourself, and second, it will let you know it will take a very long time to conquer your real foe, yourself. The end result should provide you with incentive to become more tolerant with your wife or husband or significant other and your friends and neighbors, not to forget those "hypocrites" at the local church.

In any relationship there must be give and take. Acceptance takes the day, mainly because both of the parties involved have faults. There must be a commitment to excellence which won't take place overnight. The following three poems sum up the vital elements involved in a relationship, faith, hope and love:

Watch It Rain

Noah got the news, a directive,
"Now see here, this is our objective",
So by faith he builds a boat on ground,
While the world laughs and says he is not sound,
Yet his family and animals by two,
Boarded the ark when he was all through;

And he prayed aloud, without raising Cain,
"Step back non-believer; watch it rain."

Life got all messed and tossed me away,
Broke and no job, tears from day to day,
In the ashes of my ruin I sat,
Till another came to help, my back to pat,
And by faith we began a new life,
While knowing in the days ahead, strife,
But began with a goal, in the main,
"Step back non-believer; watch it rain."

We've had financial loss, some by theft,
We had each other, so not bereft,
Made the wilderness come alive, even bloom,
Optimistic and happy, not gloom,
Made each day count, our every quest,
Love with abandon, be our very best,
And say amid our personal gain,
"Step back non-believer; watch it rain."

The Magic Wishing Well

Each day the maiden came to the magic wishing well,
To drink deeply from its cool water then sit a spell,
She wandered midst the garden, each treat a fresh delight,
With wonders there she would forever hold in her sight.
There were pomegranates and dewberries off the vine,
Clusters of rich, white grapes that some day would become wine,
Almonds and pecans by the handful, easy to shell,
Succulent peaches, where they come from no one could tell,
And the splendor of the magic lingered until night,
Then off she went on her way by early, evening light.

Some often wonder, with regret, wherein their youth went,
When they look upon their lives with their days nearly spent,
But the maiden with the magic wishing well now past,
In her memories she ever holds so dear and fast;
Knows the revelry she had found in those bygone days,
With the richness and joy given through its magic ways,
So every new day she finds riches to explore,

To soar with the bluebirds their gifts of grace to implore,
And to forever hold in her heart that trysting place,
With strength to cope, to endure, to run her final race

Take Me to the River

Gather round, sinners, gather round,
I feel a sermon coming down,
The topic will be sin, which I am ag'in.
"Let me take you to the river; drop you in the water,
Take you to the river; put you in the water…"

When you are sick, or just not sound,
Or, when life gets you down,
Like Jonah and the whale, and Noah and the ark,
What'd they do when things looked so dark?
Man, they said, "Take me to the river; drop me in the water,
Take me to the river; put me in the water…"

What if you longed for your mate all day long?
But when she got home something went wrong,
Yea, you'd been thinking of nothing but her,
And all you got was a grrrr,
You say, "Take me to the river; drop me in the water,
Take me to the river; put me in the water…"

But on the other hand things go just right,
And yeah, you know that this is the night,
Touching her softly as you brush by,
She looks at you with a gleam in her eye,
You sing, "Take me to the river; drop me in the water,
Take me to the river; put me in the water…"

Please notice in the last poem I have equated love with the wife as the highest norm. Your beloved holds that place; don't lose it. Ah amore, amore, amore! When you have a deep love here, you will know how to love others as well.

Each of these lifestyles offers a comfort zone. They may even provide one with a cozy little life, all wrapped up neatly in their security blanket from childhood. Perhaps the position also tells them they are okay; many often feel they are doing 'good,' so there comes no change in one's stance;

unless, however, a hell-fire and brimstone preacher turns them inside out. Without a true conversion they then disguise themselves in sheep's clothing; only their family knows for sure. Even Saddam feels amid the killing and plundering he does what is best for Iraq. There is a good chance one will have a deep desire to change if he or she meets the right cause. The conversion takes a lifetime to accomplish.

For the Christian, the cause comes in the person of Jesus Christ. Let's look at Matthew 20:25-28 to begin our review:

> "But Jesus called them to him and said, "You know the rulers of the Gentiles lord it over them, and their great men exercise authority over them. It shall not be so among you; but whoever would be great among you must be your servant, and whoever would be first among you must be your slave; even as the Son of man came not to be served but to serve, and to give his life as a ransom for many". (NIV)

The word ransom means to free one from servitude (Cf. Dr. Malcolm Tolbert, "Good News From Matthew"). Cain is free; yet he still needs to become free from his passions. Freedom means to have a higher purpose in life than mere existence. If we are to hold the mantle of Christ, we shall become a minister. Again, I will refer the reader back to the section on significance, where the ultimate meaning of minister is not our position or striving for a position, but our calling. Everyone is called to be a minister, to live in freedom from our quest to be something in superficial categories. Freedom requires a lifestyle, not some specific thing you do. What you do comes from within. Rather, what you are becoming in Christ. Remember the words of God to Moses, "I am becoming!"

Next the Question arises, "To whom was the ransom paid?"(See, A Theological Word Book of the Bible" edited by Alan Richardson). There are three theories presented through the years which we shall now observe. The first thought set forth comes from the "ransom" concept, which has Jesus paying the Devil for our souls. Satan, thinking he has won, swallows the death of Jesus as a victory, only to see the tables turn on him. The second requires Jesus to soothe the feathers of a ruffled God because Adam and Eve disobeyed him in the beginning. This is called the "penal" doctrine of the cross. Here the idea is to redeem man from an injured God who seeks justice. Jesus then passes the boon on to man since he has nothing to gain; he is perfect so he gives us a free pass. The third idea has more to do with ourselves. Jesus' death presents a challenge to us to awaken the dormant power in us to overcome our own drives and egotistical endeavors. Once we "see" (revelation) the concept, we are inevitably drawn to it.

I am grateful to Joseph Campbell for this insight "Creative Mythology, pg35):

> "The ultimate ground of the individual character, …lies beyond research, beyond analysis; it is in the body of the individual as it comes to birth. Hence, the circumstances of the environment in which the individual lives do not determine the character. They provide only the furtherances and hindrances of its temporal fulfillment, as do soil and rain the growth and flowering of seed. "The experiences and illuminations of childhood and early youth…become in later life the types, standards and patterns of all subsequent knowledge and experience, or as it were, the categories according to which all later things are classified—not always consciously, however. And so it is that in our childhood years the foundation is laid of our later view of the world, and therewith as well of its superficiality or depth; it will be in later years unfolded and fulfilled, not essentially changed" (Campbell here quoted Schopenhauer).
>
> "The inborn, or, as Schopenhauer terms it, intelligible character is unfolded only gradually and imperfectly through circumstance; and what comes to view in this way he calls the empirical (experienced or observed) character. Our neighbors, through observation of this empirical character, often become more aware than ourselves of the intelligible, innate personality that is secretly shaping our life. We have to learn though experience what we are, want, and can do,, and "until then," declares Schopenhauer, we are characterless, ignorant of ourselves, and have often to be thrown back onto our proper way by hard blows from without. When finally we shall have learned, however, we shall have gained what the world calls 'character'—which is to say, earned character. And this, in short, is neither more nor less than the fullest possible knowledge of our own individuality."

In order to get this 'earned' degree, we have to pass muster, this is to have this compelling Christ to call us out of our 'garden bed' to compassion.

The disciples come away from the crucifixion empty. Until they 'see' the example in its revealed light, they sit in darkness.

> In Luke 24:13-32 (RSV) we read:
> "That very day two of them were going to a village named Emmaus about seven miles from Jerusalem, and talking with each other about all these thing that had happened. While they were talking and discussing together, Jesus himself drew near and went with them. But their eyes were kept from recognizing him. And he said to them, "What is this conversation which you are holding with each other as you walk?"
> And they stood still, looking sad. Then one of them, named Cleopas, answered him "Are you the only visitor to Jerusalem who does not know the things that have happened there in these days?" And he said to them, "What things?" And they said to him, "Concerning Jesus of Nazareth, who was a prophet mighty in deed and word before God and all the people, and how our chief priests and rulers delivered him up to be condemned to death, and crucified him. But we had hoped that he was the one to redeem Israel.
> Yes, and besides all this, it is now the third day since this happened. Moreover, some women of our company amazed us. They were at the tomb early in the morning and did not find his body; and they came back saying that they had even seen a vision of angels, who said that he was alive. Some of those who sere with us went to the tomb, and found it just as the women had said; but him they did not see."
> And he said, "O foolish men, and slow of heart to believe all that the prophets have spoken! Was it not necessary that the Christ should suffer these things and enter into his glory?" And beginning with Moses and all the prophets, he interpreted to them in all the scriptures the things concerning himself.
> So they drew near to the village to which they were going. He appeared to be going further, but they constrained him saying, "Stay with us, for it is toward evening and the day is now far spent." So he went in to stay with them. When he was at table with them, he took the bread, and broke

it, and gave it to them. And they recognized him; and he vanished out of their sight."

Paul had a cataclysmic experience on the Damascus road. Whatever he 'saw', it changed his life. Ever after he declared Jesus was the way. More, he proclaimed from jail:

> "…as it is my eager expectation and hope that I shall not be at all ashamed, but that with full courage now as always Christ will be honored in my body, whether by life or by death. For me to live is Christ, and to die is gain. If it is to be life in the flesh, that means fruitful labor for me. Yet which I shall choose I cannot tell. I am hard pressed between the two. My desire is to depart and be with Christ, for that is far better. But to remain in the flesh is more necessary on your account" (Phil 1:20-24).

As Hamlet mused, "To be or not to be that is the question"(Act 3; Scene 1)? For Paul, his life was directed to grasp the one who had grasped him. Indeed, to be or not to be is the question for all who take the name of Christ. Where is compassion? Where is brotherly love? In the church we grab for power and position to feed our egos while the world starves for love and understanding. The very nature of the revelation, and it is revelation, not historical fact, the first believers came to understand their calling in the nature and will of God for the meaning and destiny of life.

If we see the same thing they saw, should we not say, "To whom shall we go; only you have the words for eternal life?" This new found freedom is life, a gift of God to be lived in trying to grasp the one who grasped us. It requires a new type of individual who will (Cf. Erich Fromm, "You Shall Be As Gods," pg 57ff):

1. Think outside the bun.
2. Think on things that are pure and noble
3. Think not that things are a means to an end. Self is the only end we should change, not others.
4. Think to curb the ego; kill narcissism.
5. Think transcendence; to this end we shall return in the final chapter.

Any true thought, whether from Jesus or from poetic imagery, should bring us to The center of Markham's circle; there we meet self, God and others.

God's Celestial Shore

There is a land of which I am aware,
A holy Eden filled with constant care,
I am but a traveler on my way,
Along with you my friend every day.
Trails, some vicious, come often on the trail,
To remind me of myself, only frail,
But I know heavenly bowers do shade,
The road I run in my motorcade,
In this our splendid land that I adore,
On my way to God's celestial shore.
The highest honor is love another,
Live out your life with the holy other,
To amble, to share, to traverse the vale,
And with that special one yourself avail;
Know the value of the one you adore,
Always seek well being and good explore,
And in all of these things you'll find true love,
The happiness you desire from above,
Daily riches before that special door,
Which leads to God's celestial shore.
How you will arrive is important too,
To achieve the worth expected of you;
Catch each day the splendor of God's array,
Sunset, evening star, bluebirds on their way,
The newness of morn, the sweet kiss of dew,
Promises to keep, more than just a few;
So at night you can really say adieu,
When you've filled it with all you meant to do,
Then you will know the everlasting more,
Liken to yon God's celestial shore.

The Pumpkin Patch

Everyone remembers the story of "Cinderella". The magical myth has been recreated in many ways, including a Jerry Lewis movie, "Cinderfella". At mid-night the carriage turns into a pumpkin. Just as in the story, our magical moments in the garden passed into the harsh realities of life. I suggest that we recreate some magical moments of our own. We need to keep the magic in our lives, not so much as an escape, but an outlet or release from stress and tension. We need to let the air out, so to speak. What is wrong with having some fun? We must let our inner child out to play, in order to not grow stale and die, or worse; we get swallowed in every day life until we become our old selves again, bedraggled by cumbersome details which lead to living in a rut, with old habits that are hard to break. I am aware that Fromm has labeled much of our society as a fun-grasping society. He says:

> "Man's happiness today consists in "having fun." Having fun lies in the satisfaction of consuming and "taking in" commodities, sights, food, drinks, cigarettes, people, lectures, books, movies—all are consumed, swallowed. The world is one great object for our appetite, a big apple, a big bottle, a big breast; we are the sucklers, the eternally expectant ones, the hopeful ones—and the eternally disappointed ones … (The Art of Loving).

I can agree with him if he means the things we do are an end in themselves. If we are bored, if this is all we have, then I agree. However, if our happiness comes from within, then what is wrong with grabbing a little gusto? Each moment is, to use the phrase again, an 'existential moment.'

The French have a saying, "Laissez les bon temps rouler." It means let the good times roll. At times we are saddened that the blissful moments have come to an end. We face a lonely moment when this happens. Therefore we must have something more in the tank; a raison d'être. At other times, we are glad they are over, like when the company leaves so you can relax, catch your breath before you clean up the mess. What I am saying is to let your creative side express itself from time to time. Enjoy life; feel free to do so. When the child dies, the staid, old parent offers little entertainment, if any.

When the Circus Comes to Town

I sat alone on the bench along the sidelines,
Rehearsing my script, saying by rote the lines,
Until the day the circus came to town;
And then the happiness I found.
They raised the poles for their tents two stories high,
Hung the ropes so the trapeze artists could fly,
Nailed down the pegs with hammers large,
People working orders from someone in charge;
They were small, large, fat and freaky women and men,
And I couldn't wait to hear their story, to see where they'd been.

In no time the tents were up and the show began;
Riders on horses with banners carrying their slogan,
All in costumes of all colors in a splendid array,
And then the Wild West show to set the tone for the day.
In one ring the lion tamer faced a beast pawing the sand;
Ring two had an elephant raise himself on one foot on a tiny stand,
While in the center ring a man walked on the high wire,
And other flew through the air and tossed his mate tough a ring of fire;
All the time I watched, amazed, eating my cracker jacks;
Cotton candy, apples on a stick and popcorn from long, white sacks.

Then intermission and I thought things would get dull.
Entered the clown, and that ended the lull.
Funny face, with a huge red nose, and orange colored wig,
The largest feet I'd ever seen, and pok-a-dot pants way too big,
And I would laugh and play until the M.C. did bark,
Then the whole place ended up in the dark.
Suddenly a multicolored light beamed on the center ring,

117

Announcing the coming attraction like when a diva would sing,
And the breath-taking feat I'd go over and over in the night;
And long for the morrow, to once again behold those things in my sight;
Then I realized, one day they would bring the big top down,
And oh the sadness I'd feel, if the circus ever left town.

On the other hand, when the things that we do for entertainment become a means to an end, then we end up with nothing. This is exactly to what Fromm meant in his criticism above. Take the following poem for example (See Gayley; from "The Satyr," by Robert Buchanan):

"The trunk of this tree,
Dusky-leaved, shaggy-rooted,
Is a pillow well suited,
To a hybrid like me,
Goat-bearded, goat-footed;
For the boughs of the glade
Meet above me, and throw
A cool, pleasant shade
On the greenness below;
Dusky and brown'd
Close the leaves all around;
And yet, all the while,
Thro' the boughs I can see
A star, with a smile,
Looking at me . . .
Why, all day long,
I run about
With a madcap throng,
And laugh and shout.
Silenus grips
My ears, and strides
On my shaggy hips,
And up and down
In an ivy crown
Tipsily rides;
And when in doze
His eyelids close,
Off he tumbles, and I
Can his wine-skin steal,
I drink—and feel

The grass roll — sea high;
Then with shouts and yells,
Down mossy dells,
I stagger after
The wood-nymphs fleet,
Who with mocking laughter
And smiles retreat;
And just as I clasp
A yielding waist,
With a cry embraced,
—Gush! It melts from my grasp
Into water cool,
And—bubble! Trouble!
Seeing double!
I stumble and gasp
In some icy pool!"

What better place to start our journey through the World's Fair than the wedding. Talk about a magical time. I've held weddings in large and small churches, chapels, river banks, in front of fireplaces, VFW halls, AMVETS, Knights of Columbus halls, before an old barn and in my back yard. They all have the same ingredients. There is magic everywhere. Some require more elaborate planning; while some need no planning at all. Underneath the moment lies the great expectation. Anticipation abounds. In the larger weddings, both sides of the family gets involved in the pre-game warm ups and the reception for the winners. The realization of having been in the midst of this excels the boundaries of the ones participating, most especially the lovers. Exhilaration covers up the expense, the constant going and the planning to make sure everything turns out swell. During the warm up the night before, concerns weigh heavily on the mother of the bride that all will go well. While the event unfurls, things happen which she will only laugh at herself for being concerned because the odd things only make the occasion more memorable.

In my admonitions, no matter the place, I like to compare this event to the Garden of Eden. There the first couple find themselves before God who will unite them in marital bliss. God tells them to become one, to cleave to each other; he tells them to leave home to make a place for themselves. Their job is to be fruitful and multiply; to find happiness in each other. Becoming one means to have intimacy, sexually as well as mentally. How is that for left and right brain union? The two become one yet remain two as we see in the following poems:

"Marriage is the union of two divinities that a third might
be born on earth.
It is the union of two souls in a strong love for abolishment
of separateness.
It is the higher unity which fuses the separate unities
within the two spirits.
It is the golden ring in a chain, whose beginning is a
glance,
and whose ending is Eternity.
It is the pure rain that falls from an unblemished sky to
fructify
And bless the fields of divine Nature."

Kahlil Gibran "Secrets of the Heart"

A marriage is born of love and should grow in love. Love does not question; it knows. Love does not hesitate; it acts. Love is not only affinity and attraction; it is union. Love makes two people indispensable to each other.

"Love one another, but make not a bond of love;
Let it rather be a moving sea between the shores of your
souls.
Fill each other's cup but drink not from one cup.
Give one another of your bread but eat not from the same
loaf.
Sing and dance together and be joyous, but let each one
of you be alone,
Even as the strings of a lute are alone though they quiver
with the same music."

Kahlil Gibran "The Prophet"

The husband-wife relationship is intended to be at its best one of mutual love and respect, with neither one dominating the other. With the birth of children from such a union, a mysterious, creative relationship with the Creator can be discerned.

The finale comes when I remind them it is 11:59, P.M. The vows they take here end the storybook affair. Of course I know the honeymoon is part of the deal; but it comes to an abrupt end also. The real tests come in the day-to-day relationships where they should try to discover what the vows means; they should try to work out these vows each day they live for this day is over; there is only tomorrow, tomorrow, tomorrow. . . More, they should strive to keep the magic of this love alive, for in it they will achieve heaven. They can't return here ever again, but they can go back to renew, to remember and to revive the magic there. Merle Haggard probably says it best:

> "I guess everything does change except what you choose to recall;
>   There's a million good daydreams to dream on,
>   But Baby, you are my favorite memory of all."

The next stop will be at the mall. Shopping is a real chore for some. I like to think of shopping as fun. Besides it gives us a sense of power like we have never had before. Think about the times you purchased a home, a car, a new boat or some piece of equipment for the home of yard. You felt good about being able to buy the item. The only thing, it will not last, the euphoric feeling. The house gets too small; the car becomes too passé; the lawn equipment wears out; and the computer gets out of date. Hence the let down comes.

I guess what I am trying to get across is that in shopping you find the anticipation of the event is the expectation of the coming attraction. This becomes the splendor of shopping, the power to be overlords to things. We can go down the aisle in quest of those needed things to buy, and if we have the money, we can pick up a few things to surprise the family when we get home. Buying something to bring home for the wife, kids or pets adds a rich luster to the spree. It no longer is a chore; it is a delightful moment in our lives, separating us from the daily rut for a while.

The down side to shopping and buying things, if they become an endless search for happiness, they will let you down. In the movie, "Cat On a Hot Tin Roof", Big Daddy learns he has a terminal illness. He goes into the cellar to be alone. His son, with whom he has been at odds, goes to meet him. In the course of the conversation the son observes the vast amount of stored objects or 'things'. He asks Big Daddy what in the world did he intend to do with all the items, some of whom had not even been touched. Big Daddy replies, "Your Momma had me buy them. I kept buying those things for her in hopes that I might find in them eternal life. Not so!" And so it is.

The day after Christmas in 2003, a lady was in the line ahead of me at Wal-Mart's. She had purchased $194.00 worth of items that had been placed on sale. She had all her relatives' names on them mentally. When it came time to pay, there was not enough money in her account, so she put some back. After the new cost arrived, she still was short. She kept putting things back until she got down under a hundred dollars. By this time the cashier was getting a little harried, although she kept her cool. She called the manager over to help. In the final analyses, she didn't have enough money in her account to pay for the coke she had purchased. All she did was laugh. She exclaimed, "I had fun while it lasted." And I had fun watching the show.

Probably more than any other thing, other than sex, the way we spend our money, or lack of money, will cause more hardships within the family, especially a newly wed. I am not saying to spend recklessly, but plan to spend and have fun doing it. After the thrill is gone, the routine of the monthly bills comes rolling into the valley. The point remains, we have control of this venture, like no other time in our lives. It does point us to the celestial shore. Again, it is not an end in itself.

Another way to find bliss amidst the hardships of life comes in the form of festivals that commemorate some special event or ethic of the people where the event occurs. Also, there are special town and cities that have attractions to see to experience the thrill of the culture. I think little Mamou, La. would be the epitome of what I say. They have a major attraction each Saturday, and only on Saturday does Fred's open. The Cajun culture with the accordion and French music leaps out at you. You don't want the morning to end because they close at one o'clock P.M. until the next week. Yet hundreds come every week to attend. The place won't hold much more than 100, but it is always crowded.

I like the smaller events, but each to his own. In Louisiana we have hundreds of festivals including the major one, Mardi Gras. You can get lost in wonder and amazement there. Think of this as the bliss of the very essence of our hopes and dreams. Everyone parties. They all see each other as one. There are no stereotypes there. The visitors who just come to see the show only look with amazement at the revelers. In the main, all have something to tell when they get back home.

The Painted Pony

Fantasies were lost with the coming of fall,
Reading, writing and 'rithmetic would recall,
But given time, lady luck brought back the fun,
An escape from the routine, a chance to run,
As the midway beckoned, seals barking their spiels,
Pandas in all sizes, bright shiny eyes, gave thrills,
Each pleading, reaching for you to take them home,
Throw darts, toss the ball, shoot the ducks made of chrome;

Candied apples, car'mel corn, cotton candy,
The smell of fresh hay from the barn so handy,
And I, I would catch the painted pony and ride, ride, ride. . .

I helped in a fashion show in 2003 where nothing but cancer survivors were the models. The experience taught me a valuable lesson. All of them had a zest for life that had been sharpened by the possibility of their impending death. Several of the men had just returned from a trip to Memphis. They told of their visit to 'Beale Street' and of the fun they had there. I had been to Memphis as well, but they made me think my time there had been mundane. They saw things I had not. They thrilled at every song, every morsel of food and each unique shop they entered. They saw the hotel where the ducks hang out, although they didn't stay there. When they returned to their hotel they asked a lady if she had been to 'Beale Street' and she said no. Then they asked her if she had even seen the ducks and she said, "I am too busy with my church; I don't have time to visit." It did them little good to try to tell her to smell the roses.

Vacations are up to the individual taste as well as a busman's holiday. In the Marine Corps we call that a week-end of R&R. Time off from the routine means special times which fill up endless home movies, scrapbooks and etc. I enjoy the two or three days visits because you always have to return before you are ready. The opposite of that is the one that you are ready to go home long before the allotted time to go home comes.

Please forgive me for including another personal injection, but B. J. and I love to go to Galveston to fish off the pier and most of all, we love to go to New Orleans for a day or two. We eat in the most delightful places, sit to watch the ball game at some bar and dance to the local jazz, Cajun or blues bands. From time to time we take the river boat for a night cruise, not to eat, but listen and dance to the music; or we lean over the side outside to just watch the magic of the night with the lights and the moon dancing on the river.

Similar to this is the week-end movie or rent one from the local rental. Cook outs with friends or just the family making life a pleasure always has been a favorite of mine. I remember the times with my mother and step-father when we boiled shrimp or crawfish. We had corn, potatoes and the main entrée with plenty to drink. Often we had friends over to partake of the festive occasion. Those times are treats that can happen at any given time at home with only the mess to clean up afterward.

An intimate meal or one with family or friends brings to mind special occasions which one should plan on doing as often as possible. If you are on a limited income, the lady of the house knows how to squeeze a little back to make this come true. Again B.J. and I make this happen each day to plan and to cook something together. Before and after the meal we have long intimate talks to express the events of the day or discuss something we read in the paper or some good book we read recently.

The Painted Pony

Day finds me at my task, sometimes in a lull,
While by the seashore, someone admires a gull,
And I long for ev'ning, my life to renew,
Have a seat with my lover, the day to review,
To take in the splendor, wonders God has wrought,
Finding freedom from tyranny which we've fought,
Acute sounds of the night will be on display,
Birds of red, blue and gray, with ring necks at play,
The western view, white on blue and golden hue,
Some wine, man's best friend and especially you,
And I, I will catch the painted pony and ride, ride, ride. . .

We cook on special holidays, but often the children have other stops to make. We want them to know we understand, but if they are coming, we usually fry a turkey with all the trimmings. Holidays are special because the family and friends can get together. B.J.'s youngest son hunted Easter eggs at our house until he graduated from med-school. There is nothing wrong in keeping Santa, the Easter Bunny and the Tooth Fairy alive in your life. This just makes life rich and enjoyable. I don't understand someone getting tied up with a staid ole religion that prohibits any real fun. My Catholic friends know how to have fun without guilt. The Cajun culture calls for injection of the good things that make the world a better place to live. Don't be mistaken, true friends like you as a person regardless if you are in the money or broke, they just like you. Too many friendships come about by money or prestige; the true friend loves you for being you. It's not the money.

The Cajuns have a legend about Parlangue, a half-man and half-alligator. I take this to mean the oneness with nature and one another. The symbolism extends beyond any given boundaries to indicate the mores and festive life which they enjoy. Most of my life I have lived among them to see the special relationship they have through the cultural adaptation of their lives. We should have a motto: No Boundaries!

In the same vein, Hawthorne saw the Marble Faun of Praxiteles which ensnared him the rest of his life. It, too, was a symbol of a baroque society;

but Hawthorne contrasted it over the staid Puritan, Victorian religion of his ancestors. His character Donatello represented the faun until guilt took the life out of him. When he expelled his guilt, he was recalled to life like Monsieur Manette was recalled from prison to new life in Dickens', "A Tale of Two Cities". At that time Donatello could accept the consequences of his actions. Even if he went to prison, he had found true freedom.

The next item I would like to bring up is sex. I am not Dr. Ruth nor do I have a scheme to make you successful. I only know that sex is wholesome and it adds zest to your life. If you have problems with your sexual appetite, always hungry or no hunger at all, see a doctor. Make sex a happy part of your life. I believe in wholesome sex between consenting adults. Teens should learn to wait until they can be responsible with their own appetites, not hidden in some closest. Make plans to have an intimate night with your wife or partner. Treat her with the same desire you did when you were chasing her. She will love the chase. Of course, the spontaneous times are fun as well. When you choose a mate, you have chosen him or her for life. There is no reason you can't have this relationship until you are too old to care.

I have friends in their eighties who still enjoy sex. My grandfather claims he could ring the bell when he was 85, but I know better. He and grandmother slept in twin beds and the walls were paper thin. Besides, she wanted to do so and he turned her down because it might make her ill, since she was sickly anyway. I say this to mean it is possible and it should be a dream of everyone to do so, unless hindered physically. With all the wonder drugs out now, men who lacked potency years ago would love to be alive now.

Some years ago a young lady came to me for advice. She had a problem with oral sex. Her husband wanted it, but she didn't. I told her that was something each had to work out, and they should discuss the issue. If he insisted against her wishes, then he didn't realize the delicate side of her nature. He didn't bother to find out what she liked. However, after talking with her, I found out her mother did not like sex because of various inhibitions stemming from her childhood. Mainly, the lady's problem stemmed from religion which said this act was taboo and she felt dirty doing it. Whether she had passed on the knowledge to her daughter knowingly I was not sure. Only until she rid herself from these taboos will she ever enjoy sex to the fullest. After having justification from an open minded person, if she still didn't like the other, she needed to have a mate who understood that there is more to sex than that.

Merle Haggard has a song that goes like this:

"Let's chase each other round the room tonight;
Let's play the games we played on our wedding night;
To lock and close the door is only right,
Let's chase each other round the room tonight.
Seems like lately people love to play with fire;
The other games they play are just as bad;
I'd rather stay at home and feel your burning lips
And play the kind of games that make me glad. . .
Let's don't chase and make each other weary;
Let's keep all our love at home and out of sight;
Let's keep everything like jealousy behind us;
And let's chase each other round the room tonight."

In the Garden of Eden God tells the couple to become one. There sex is good for all God created was good. Man and woman are to live out their lives in the flesh with wholesome sex. History shows that throughout the years sex has become cheapened by prudish, small minded individuals which sought to lead us from the garden principle. There is a sexual revolution going on, and more power to it. As long as union between two people shows an expression of their joy in each other it lends itself to the nurture of mutual humanity. When mankind uses sex to manipulate and to tear down and to dominate, it becomes cheap and tawdry.

In our lifetime we have seen our young men and women go off to war. One of the happiest times comes when they return home, hopefully unscathed. Still, even if they have had misfortune, everyone, especially the family, rejoices because they are alive. I remember my uncle coming home from WWII, walking down the dusty road with his duffle bag on his shoulder. The whole house was ablaze with excitement; it was like Christmas, only we were more expectant, if you can imagine such a thing. My brother and I went to bed around midnight, but the rest of the family stayed awake all night talking and celebrating his return.

I think of another story where a Vietnamese lady had lost two of her sons in the Viet Nam war prior to this occasion. The news came to her that the third son had been killed. Someone asked how she was coping, and the answer came, "She is standing alone in apparent shock; but she stands tall like a tree, swaying but not broken." Our hearts went out to her.

These are mixed reactions, but the prayer of everyone is that all will return safely, but life doesn't always afford us our wishes. I am grateful for all the parades and the honor bestowed on those who returned home from the Iraqi war; I am also grateful to those who gave the ultimate sacrifice for freedom and my love goes out to the families who suffer much in these trying times.

There are many times when you can find a once in a life time experience. You can't relive them, but you can rekindle the flame. In 2003 several of the old gang got together to reminisce and to swap tales, mostly to adlib and to see whom could embellish the past the most. It was a very joyous occasion to visit with the guys with whom I had spent many hours of my youth. The greatest thing about the visit, we still had fond memories of each other which through the years had not waned although we had not seen each other for thirty and some odd years. If a person has one friend, he is lucky. If by chance he has more than one, he is really blessed.

Earlier in the year of 2003, my step-father died to which it was my privilege to do the honors at his service. The most important thing came after the wake when the whole family, down to the great grandchildren, came together as one. We had forgotten the old wounds and hurts we had caused each other; we truly came together to love and appreciate one another, maybe for the very first time. Times like these are precious and few. Perhaps it made us more aware to do more of the 'getting together.'

I knew you wanted to know about the mark. Yes, he had it, but he was an existential person with no fear. His problem was he never learned compassion for the weaker person. He was more of the Cro-Magnon male who could not show weakness by being emotional or crying. Woman's place was doing the 'feeling' thing. He did teach me two things that I will never forget. He taught me to be myself no matter the circumstances, although he would not let me be myself for a long time. It is okay to be yourself, but you don't have to flaunt it. The second thing he taught me was if I 'gotta' be me, then I had to let others be themselves. The following song by Frank Sinatra summed up his life:

"And now the end is near, and so I face the final curtain,
My friend, I'll say it clear; I'll state my case of which I'm certain;
I lived a life that's full; I traveled each and every highway;
And more, much more than this, I did it my way."

Transcendence

In December of 2003, Dodge comes out with a new advertisement about their new Durango. The young couple drives off the lot with their small child in the rear seat. On the way home the wife tells the young person all about the 'feminine' features which enticed her to agree to buy. When they get home, the father opens the hood to show the child the motor; then he says, "Here is all you need too know. It's a Hemi; can you say Hemi?" The child then says, "Hemi!"

This typifies the thinking of the left brain and right brain usage I have written about earlier. I now wish to move on to show a level of thinking which will lead us to higher ground. In our every day mode of living, much of the thinking is done from the left side where the left brain takes control choosing logic, reasoning and details over the imagination and artistic talent of the right side. This means that most people will never reach their maximum potential because of the continual usage of the left side. We have to train ourselves to think another way. The following ideas are not set before us as a guide; neither do I think that I have all the answers nor do I think I have arrived. I only hope the ideas set forth help me to get to my destination as well.

The following article came to me during the time of the writing of this manuscript via e-mail. I feel obliged to copy it because it takes us toward the road we are to travel. This is man's message to women. You can turn it around to see the distance men have to go to get to thinking with the right side of the brain. Here goes:

"Learn to work the toilet seat. You're a big girl. If it is up, put it down. We need it up, you need it down. You don't hear us complaining about you leaving it down.

Sunday sports. It's like the full moon or the changing of the tides, Let it be.

Shopping is not a sport. And no, we are never going to think of it that way.

Crying is blackmail.

Ask for what you want. Let us be clear on this one: Subtle hints do not work! Strong hints do not work! Obvious hints do not work! Just say it.

Yes and no are perfectly good answers.

Come to us with a problem only if you want help solving it. That's what we do. Sympathy is what your girlfriends are for.

A headache that lasts for 17 months is a problem. See a doctor.

Anything we said 6 months ago is inadmissible in an argument. In fact, all comments become null and void after 7 days.

If you want dress like the Victoria's Secret girls, don't expect us to act like soap opera guys.

If you think you are fat, you probably are. Don't ask.

If something we said can be interpreted two ways, and one of the ways makes you sad or angry, we meant the other one.

You can either ask us to do something or tell us how you want it done. Not both. If you already know best how to do it, just do it yourself.

Whenever possible, please say whatever you have to say during commercials.

Christopher Columbus did not need directions and neither do we.

All men see in only 16 colors, like Windows default settings. Peach is a fruit. Pumpkin is a fruit. We have no idea what mauve is.

If it itches, it will be scratched. We do that.

If we ask what is wrong and you say "nothing," we will act like nothing's wrong.

If you ask a question you don't want an answer to, expect an answer you don't want to hear.

When we have somewhere to go, absolutely anything you wear is ok… Really.

You have enough clothes; you have too many shoes.

I am in shape. Round is a shape."

All of these are some of the every day issues between the opposite sexes. They are included here just for fun to set the stage for the coming events. They are not meant for a prototype individual, especially to indicate all men are typical.

Now I present the woman's side of the story. I received this e-mail from a male friend who knows the worth of a woman. Here goes (Copied as is, unedited):

"Women have strengths that amaze men. They bear hardships and they carry burdens. They smile when they want to scream. They sing when they want to cry. They cry when they are happy and laugh when they are nervous. They fight for what they believe in. They stand up to injustice. They don't take "no" for an answer when they believe there is a better solution. They go without so their family can have. They go to the doctor with a frightened friend. They love unconditionally. They cry when their children excel and cheer when their friends get awards. They are happy when they hear about a birth or a wedding. Their hearts break when a friend dies. They grieve at the loss of a family member, yet they are strong when they think there is no strength left. They know that a hug and a kiss can help to heal a broken hart. Women come in all sizes, in all colors and shapes. They'll drive, fly, walk, run or e-mail you to show how much they care about you. The heart of a woman is what makes the world keep turning! They bring joy and hope. They have compassion and ideals. They give moral support to their family and friends. Women have vital things to say and everything to give."

The unknown author goes on to say, "However, if there's one flaw in women, it is that they tend to forget their worth." Perhaps it is the other way around; the men forget to realize women's worth by taking them for granted.

In the Garden of Eden, God gives the couple some important advice. If we are to begin thinking with both sides of our brain, we must consider the relationship between the married couple as the most important guide to transcendence between souls. If we can't make it work here, how can we make it work in our everyday relationships? These admonitions are not in any order; and none have priority over the others. First let's consider the woman as a help-mate to Adam. If she is a help-mate, does not this make Adam a helper's mate? I think so. There is nothing wrong with the male helping around the house. Today there are more women in the work force than ever before. Women go into battle with a gun in recent wars which was not the case many years ago.

Try thinking, okay girl, I am going to try to make your work a little easier. In fact I will learn to cook, take turns with the baby, share the remote and talk to you on a deeper level. Spend time sharing before getting on the couch. Years ago the man sits in the living room watching TV while the wife does the evening meal. I can see the opposite happening now. And why not? If she had a very hard day, give her the evening off. You tell her you love her; do you mean it?

Another guide from the garden comes from God himself. He tells the young Adam to leave his father and mother to cleave to his wife to become one with her. There are really two things here. A person has to cut the umbilical cord once more when they marry. It is okay to visit and to love your parents; but you must not allow them to dominate your lives. They have brought you into the world to love, not to control you. They have to give you up to allow you to reach the stars. Perhaps you may even go higher than they went; they should allow you to do so. In addition you must give yourself the right to do so.

The second idea here relates to intimacy. Sexual intimacy is part of the admonition. The two should learn to treat the other person with dignity and respect. To do anything to harm the unity of this relationship dishonors the sanctity of the relationship. If she is not all you want, don't marry her and vice versa. Learn what the other person's needs are; then accommodate her or him. There is nothing illegal about anything you do behind closed doors. Whatever you do, it is the highest act of love anywhere. No other act compares to it. So give mutual consent with all your love attached.

Eternal River

Love is like a river that flows endlessly,
Whose currents often twist along restlessly,
Until it reaches its last destination,
A stilling pool of peaceful restoration.

My love for you is as a winding river,
Start to finish from the eternal giver,
A soul on ice without you as my story,
To give my life meaning, its sheen and glory.

Ev'ry day its strength flows in me to render,
Releasing pure joy with radiant splendor,
Like the sun that sets with each wave a glimmer
And I afloat, no solitary swimmer.

131

Akin to this is the intimate nature of two minds coming together to create a new idea or way of thinking. You must spend time talking to understand the other person. Men can talk on the feelings level as well as women. If, they don't, they may think like the patriarchs of old who thought all women should be in their place. Look guys, a woman is a delicate work of creation; treat her that way. The point is this, if we are to begin to think everyday with both sides of the brain, we have a person of worth sleeping with us who can teach us a thing or two. By the same token, we can teach them something also. Discuss issues. If you feel he or she is stepping on your toes, back off until you can weigh both sides to reach a mature decision.

During my time of writing this book, I asked my wife for her suggestions. Believe me she had some. Sometimes I would feel like I shouldn't have done so, but after a good night's sleep I could see where she came from. There were times that she listened to me as well where she changed her mind. It is give and take, but give and take to the point where we build up the other person, not tear down.

Often couples cross swords to end up in an explosion or an all out war. One word of warning, never make a decision to act while in the 'heat of the blood'. Take time to think it out. After you cool down, you will be able to reason things out. There is nothing wrong with arguments. All couples will eventually have them because of the various imprints of their lives as well as the different ways of reasoning. What I am suggesting is to hammer out the issues intimately so that both can adjust. Besides both can learn something from the other.

This leads me to the term implode. Rather than try to cause an explosion, try to reach the inner person to build him or her to their fullest potential. My wife has taught me many things that I use in my everyday life. She has seen the potential I have; she tries to bring that out in me. I also see the creativity she has. I encourage her to use her creativity more. In all things I try to get her to let the cat out of the bag to play. She is the most loving when she does not have the cares of the world hanging on her shoulders.

I have worked cross word puzzles for years. She always said she wishes she could do them. I challenged her to do them and now she can work the ones that sometimes I can't. She just has an innate ability to know words that she tells me she didn't learn in school. I guess she got them by observation or maybe osmosis. I wrote the following poem for her on her 45th birthday:

To A Pistol

It's been said, "You were a cat at eighteen!"
And you struck out, from the nest you did wean;
True enough, the years have been productive,
You've come a long way, yet still seductive!
When life had tied you down, along came Jones,
To turn loose, to animate those tired bones.
His love has steadily grown, with passion,
With fire, like no other, in any fashion.
Also, he likes to tease, and has for years,
Kidded you about the day among your peers,
You would obtain, my dear, a certain age,
Taken out of Bob Ford's history page,
A miserable, dirty ole coward,
The one who shot that nice mister Howard,
In the back, and laid Jessie in his grave.
With none other, you can rely, Ford gave,
A bullet from his trusty forty-five;
And poor Jessie? He took one final dive.
Jessie is gone, but alas and foremost,
B.J. at forty-five won't give up the ghost.
I'm a witness and to all proclaim,
The lady has surpassed her youthful fame,
And is a person with a lot of class,
Who at any age is a gorgeous lass.
Hence, a toast, to the great times of the past,
Yet acclaim, the first will ne'er match the last!
Ergo, love and sing and dance like Astaire,
And go out baby, with your special flair.

One other thought I will leave you in regard to the marriage relationship. Martin Buber developed the theory of an I-Thou relationship with God. He could not conceive of speaking of God in the third person. I prefer to think of an 'I-thee' relationship to one's spouse (as well as other relationships). The French have two words which mean you. "Tu", is the intimate word while "vous" has a non-familiar meaning. Think of 'thee' as 'tu', if you will. See in the other person the very essence of God. God breathes into the first people to give them life. He does to each of us. Perhaps we have forgotten to remember the other person, our spouse, as our opposite self, created in God's image. The commandment of Jesus, "love thy neighbor as thy self," will become clearer when we love our 'mates' as ourselves. Rose Parsons Stokes said in "My Prayer":

> "Some pray to marry the man they love,
> My prayer will somewhat vary:
> I humbly pray to Heaven above
> To love the man I marry."

There are three Greek words for love which one needs to understand. One is 'philo' which means love for a friend. Who else is better suited to be your best friend? Your mate knows every carbuncle you have on your body and he or she still loves you. One of the greatest joys of my life is that my wife and I love to spend time together. We indeed are friends. I do not suggest your mate be your only friend, but endeavor to make the spouse holy and dear.

The next kind of love is 'eros' which needs no introduction. He is Cupid with his cute little bow and arrow. He shot you and your mate early in life. Now it is up to each to make the lifetime together a dance; you make the arrow quiver each and every day. Believe me; you will be rewarded for your efforts. We have already spoken of the sexual part of marriage, so we need go no further only to reiterate, keep young love alive.

Finally, there comes 'agape'. This loves means the kind of love which cares for the other as one who is fragile and dear. Paul discusses this kind of love in I Corinthians 13. To give you a few lines to stir your memory, I quote the following:

> "Love is patient, love is kind. It does not envy, it does not
> boast, it is not proud. It is not rude, it is not self-seeking,
> it is not easily angered, and it keeps no record of wrongs.
> Love does not delight in evil but rejoices with the truth.
> It always protects, always trusts, always hopes, always
> perseveres. . . .And now these three remain: faith, hope
> and love. But the greatest of these is love" (Vs. 4-7;13).

Love her with all your being and she will love you in return. A lady told me one time if her husband treated her like the way I described, she would honor him forever. Her preacher quickly told her the husband ruled the household and she was obliged to obey him according to Scripture. I could just see the preacher's wife, submitting to an egotistical male who probably never gave her any attention until he became horny.

The following poem sums up our quest for the perfect spouse. He or she is the one you married. Treat the other one with love, all three kinds.

The Brass Ring

Life revolves like merry-go-rounds,
Featuring many ups and downs,
While for the brass ring to extol,
We search together and we stroll,
Hand in hand down several lanes,
As the moonbeam hovers and wanes.

Each new day brings revelation,
Because you do give elation,
Making the dance an adventure;
Yet, still for the ring we venture.
"Is it here? Is it there?" we ask,
E'er so determined in our task

Then a discovery I find,
The brass ring is one of a kind,
Ne'er elusive, but e'er so near,
The holy other, you my dear,
Which darkness nor time can erase,
Life and love found throughout the chase.

I talk about 'bun' living and autonomous living in an earlier chapter. . . Many people who live inside the box are very happy. They have a very good sense of purpose for their lives. However, not all do; therefore I would like to point out some of the dangers afforded those who let others do their thinking. I think many who have an inherited religion live life in a rut. Everything stays the same. I really am thinking now though of those people making the same old mistakes over and over again. What they did yesterday will be duplicated again today and tomorrow. The way one thinks will not change as long as they fit nicely in the groove. All they have to do is look at pictures of the old home town 10 years ago and they can see everything changes but them. No wonder young people go off to school or the work place closed minded. Fromm points out in his book, "Escape From Freedom" (pg51) the two opposite poles toward which one grows encased in 'bun thinking':

> "The primary ties block his full human development; they stand in the way of the development of his reason, and his critical capacities; they let him recognize himself and others only through the medium of his, or their, participation in a clan, social or religious community, and not as human beings; in other words, they lock his development as a free, self-determining, productive individual. But although this is one aspect, there is another one. This identity with nature, clan, religion, gives the individual security. He belongs to, he is rooted in, a structuralized whole in which he has an unquestionable place. He may suffer from hunger or suppression, but he does not suffer from the worst of pains—complete aloneness and doubt."

The story of Prometheus would serve us well to review. Prometheus was one of the wisest of the Titans. He and his brother were given the privilege of giving gifts to man and to the animals. His brother gave to the animals various gifts which would enable them to survive like: strength, swiftness, feathers, fur and etc. When Prometheus sought something to give man, there was nothing left; so he took fire from the altar of the gods to give to man. Also please remember Abel took the choice portions of meat and fat to give as an offering to God. Prometheus taught man to give the worst part to the gods, covering it with fat to give it an aroma. These two things infuriated Zeus, so he gave Prometheus a special punishment. Zeus chained him to a rock; each day a vulture came to tear out his liver. At night the wound would heal; the next day the process was repeated. Zeus would have set him free if Prometheus would only tell him the name of Zeus' heir who would one day betray him. But Prometheus refused to give Zeus the answer, choosing to take the punishment until a long time later, Hercules came to kill the vulture and to release Prometheus (This story can be found on the internet).

My hat is off to all the men and women throughout the ages who had the courage to think for themselves. They are the real heroes of our past who forged onward to build this great land at the risk of losing their lives. Heroes who go to war to save our great nation from terror are abundant; sure they are afraid, but they go as volunteers to face death for you and me. They have an inner resolve that surpasses all the self made gods that we have fashioned in our own image.

During a seminar I attended in 2003, the leader gave us some of the issues insurance companies face today. One of the issues had to do with our young people coming back from the war zone with a "Post Traumatic

Stress Syndrome". This came from their being in constant danger overseas. They didn't know who would die next. When they returned to normal life, they were afraid someone was either after them or they would die suddenly; they needed counseling. Our government recognized this issue; so they provided the necessary help.

Everyone faces death. At one time or another we had the same syndrome as those returning from Iraq. Until we have the courage to face it in our lives, we will not be free to live. When we come to grips with death, we free ourselves to take risks, to live freely. Bungee jumping and sky diving are not something I care to do; some like to do those things. More power to them. Anyway, I gave them up a long time ago for one of my New Year's resolutions. I am talking about the every day occurrences where we put death totally out of mind. When we do this we are totally free to live.

By the way, there is nothing wrong with needing counseling. In fact I am reminded of the time I had all those nightmares about death and dying. I could have used some outside help myself. Only years later have I been able to muster the courage to go on living, knowing one day I will die. I believe I now have enough faith to go on courageously. Doubts, I've had a few; yet we have no choice but to trudge onward.

We have had men and women to lay down their lives to show us the way. Will we have the inner fortitude to face life like them and Prometheus and Jesus? It takes a special breed of persons to face life in the midst of suffering; in spite of circumstances they still look forward to a full and rich life. Their knowledge comes from experience, not second hand lore. They have faith in themselves which comes from the eternal creative source instilled within.

The following poem talks about the specter who rides the wind outside our windows each moment. As a child, we have the comfort of innocence, the security of being unaware, only glimpses of the dangers outside the garden. All of us desire to find the security once again we had there. Along the way we find a special place where we meet the one who tore through the gates to place the sword in the stone where none could pull it out without being called.

Connections

He rides the wind, just outside my window,
Bowling over obstacles in his way,
In the dry, arid ground of despair out there.
The monotony of the clickity-clack drones in my ear,

While the unsteady motion of my journey,
Shakes the foundation of the track I am on,
For I believe, then waver with doubt.

Dry, ugly, bones of the specter cause me to shiver,
Then sparks of light flash in my mine,
From connections singing their lullabies,
On barren trees passing swiftly by,
And I lay my head in her lap once again,
To feel the security as I did then,
And he is transformed to an angel of mercy.

The opposite of an attitude of powerlessness, isolation and questioning the meaning of one's life calls for challenge to one's perspectives. Please observe what is going on in your life. Be open to new ideas that present themselves to you. Most of all take a few risks with your life and with your beliefs. Remember, great love and great achievements require some risks. Besides what have we learned from our past mistakes? Who knows, you might just be one of the great thinkers of your age. You won't accomplish this if you hold on to old wine skins, because they won't hold new wine.

One way to observe what happens in your life is to take time to be aware of others; think not of your selfish desires to please yourself. Today people act as if they are on a fast train to Siberia; yet they never get anywhere on time. My advice column says to them and to me, "Slow down!" Ray Charles has a song out where he sings about living life in 'three/four' time. 'Take your time' does not mean to be late on your promised destinations. I don't blame parents and friends who have dinner at a specified time and the guest comes dragging in late after two hours or more. It means to leave in expectation of arriving early for appointments so that you don't have to hurry. In addition it says, "Hey, why am I rushing? I don't need to get to the mall that fast." When you go slow and you know where you are at all times, you are less likely to hurry the car in front of you when the light turns green. You won't mind standing in line at the checkout stand; or you don't mind the extra long wait at the doctor's office. Expect a delay, and you will be prepared for it without losing your cool. Besides, if you take your time you will see some unexpected joys along the way, like flowers, new homes, lights, fancy cars and perhaps see people in their environment as individuals of worth and value. I would rather have others see me in this fashion rather than to have them take out his or her frustrations on me for being a jerk.

I have in my possession a note from an anonymous friar somewhere in Nebraska. I can't reference it for you as I only have the script, so here goes:

> "If I had my life to live over, I'd try to make more mistakes next time. I would relax, I would limber up, I would be sillier than I have been this trip. I know of a very few things I would take seriously. I would be less hygienic. I would take more chances. I would take more trips. I would climb more mountains, swim more rivers and watch more sunsets. I would eat more ice cream. I would have actual troubles and fewer imaginary ones.
>
> You see, I am one of those people who lives prophylactically and sensibly and sanely, hour after hour, day after day. Oh, I have had my moments and, if I had it to do over again, I'd have more of them. In fact, I'd try to have nothing else. Just moments, one after another, instead of living so many years ahead each day. I have been one of those people who never go anywhere without a thermometer, a hot water bottle, a gargle, a raincoat and a parachute. If I had it to do over again, I would go places and do things and travel lighter than I have.
>
> If I had my life to live over again, I would start barefooted earlier in the spring and stay that way later in the fall. I would play hooky more. I wouldn't make such good grades except by accident. I would ride on more merry-go-rounds. I would pick more daisies."

It is not too late to go bare-footed in the park. Limber up. Take your time; you have only one life to live here; make it the most enjoyable you can. You owe it to yourself. When you take your time, you will find you have more time to say thank you; you will find more time to tell the waitress or clerk how helpful she was. You can make a difference in someone's day by being nice. Try it. I think you will like it.

It becomes necessary to carry the awareness idea a little further. I would like to first place you in a concentration camp. Next I am going to give you two gifts. One is the key to unlock the cell. You can come and go as often as you like. But you must go there often. Now, while you live in the camp, you will discipline yourself to learn, to read, to think, to meditate, play games, concentrate on a job you have to do and to make plans for the day, week, or month. You will also lock yourself in when you go to work each day. When you take a break, lock the door behind you. It will be permissible to discuss some of the day's events with your spouse each evening only to vent your frustrations, not to get advice. Other than this, when you come out, you have to leave all of these things behind. You must shut the door to lock them away until you return. After you leave you will be given a magnifying glass to carry with you.

I know you want to know, "Why a magnifying glass?" Because now you are free "to move about the cabin." I want you to be able to see clearly the surrounding objects and people in your life. I want them to leap out at you because you have not seen them while you were preoccupied with all the trappings you left in the camp. When you talk to your mate, you will give the other person your undivided attention. You will now see things you never saw before. In addition, when you come into the house, you will know exactly where you placed your keys, your wallet or your briefcase etc. Rather than seeing the den as a haven of rest, you will be able to see the creative nature of the decorator in your home. You will also see the mess you made; so now you become responsible to clean it up.

When you are in the world, sensitize yourself to the other people in your life. Give them your undivided attention. They will know you are listening, because they already knew when you were preoccupied when they were in your presence you paid them no mind. This will become most helpful when you have long intimate talks with your mate. Learn to listen to the words your audience says. Practice a reflective response to each statement. In other words, give some thoughts as to how you will respond. Words like, hummm; uh huh, uh huh; I see; let me get this straight, then repeat what she said; or you may do the Tim Taylor grunt.

In one of the "Home Improvement" episodes, Jill goes on television in a panel of women where she ends up trashing Tim. Of course Tim sees the show along with all of his buddies. Naturally they rib Tim. When the tool man gets home the sand hits the fan again. Jill goes to the fence to talk to Wilson. All Wilson gets to do is give her a hummm, or a grunt; she takes the reflective sound to be a solution to her dilemma; she figures out the correct course of action. Of course, Wilson is mystified because he did nothing for which she thanked him profusely for giving her advice.

One other thing, try to watch the other person mannerisms and their eyes. One commentator on Sunday afternoon football says of Tony Dungee, the coach of the Indianapolis Colts, "He teaches his guys to watch the eyes of the quarterback. The quarterback tries to hide where the ball is going, but eventually he has to see where he is throwing the ball. When he does, get ready for the play." Watching the eyes of the other person will cause you to 'hone in' on the entire conservation; it also tells the other person you are attentive. Unless the person is really sharp or aware of what he does, you can tell if he is exaggerating the story or if it is true. If his eyes go to the left, he is telling the truth. If they keep flashing to the right, he is using the right side of his brain for creativity, exaggeration or maybe lying.

The next issue I see has to do with a person denying he or she has needs. This we see in the macho man who won't let himself feel compassion or cry, especially the latter. The real person knows he or she can cry. Women don't have as big a problem as do men on this one. Everyone has needs. Some may only recognize the obvious ones that the church tries to meet like recovery after divorce, recovery after the death of a loved one, creative day care centers, meals after work or on Sunday and etc. The basic needs of one's life are the ones we describe in this text about the deep inner needs that so many people never know about or they refuse to question their motives. The truly independent person doesn't mind telling you he is a pilgrim; he or she does not know the answers; they are simply searching. They hurt; they cry; they share their questions and doubts which the 'bun' thinker may not need to do because his life fits neatly in the wrapper. Everyone should know the shortest verse in the Scripture, "Jesus wept" (John 11:35). If Jesus can weep, why can't we in this troubled word in which we live?

Anyone can be lulled into a coma by having someone tell them they are okay; this comes true when one has been baptized or partakes of the sacraments without ever having examined his or her life. Having a few rules to go by doesn't hurt them either because it adds stability to an otherwise difficult life. People can follow a few good principles adopted from the Bible, especially their pet, chosen texts which prove their case and excuse themselves from their asinine ways.

Another fallacy we fall into stems from our ability to try to blame all our problems on someone else. We need to learn to do as Orestes said, "I did it; it is my fault!" Young people today find fault with their parents, blaming them for not having enough money, not living in huge houses, not buying them a car and etc. They leave home with a stigma which will never be erased until they face up to their own shortcomings.

Don't think the adults don't have the same problems either. They become smug and satisfied. Everyone else does the sinning; and believe me, they can name their sins. Does anyone today have as a pet verse Jesus' admonition "Judge not that ye be not judged" (Matt. 7:1 KJV)? If they do, I rarely hear it.

Not long ago we had a person in our school who criticized everything the leaders did. He had no solution, but he felt like he could do a better job of running the show. After months of popping off and of constant complaining, the powers that be dismissed him. He never understood he was wrong. Consequently, he ended up a bitter person, constantly downgrading the institution.

Also, I remember in one of my early churches an elderly lady who always sat in the back pew with a kind of pious approach to life. She told me one day after the invitation was given, "Preacher, if you ever see me coming down that aisle you know I did something bad wrong." She didn't realize I knew she was on her way after church to the telephone to talk about some of the days events with the other yentas in the church. Besides, at her age I wondered what she had in mind!

One other thought before I move on to the next subject . . . Try to remember that if bad things happen to you, God does not follow you around to punish you. You just got in the way because of something you did, or you were just in 'harms way' through no fault of your own. If you are to blame, just find forgiveness to go on with your life. The autonomous thinkers know they may fail. They even make room for failure in their lives because they are willing to take a gamble now and again, or take the wrong road on occasion. We are human after all. Don't even think about saying the old Flip Wilson comedy routine, "The Devil made me do it."

Another thing I see, the 'bun' person has the answers to life's questions. They are supplied by the parent, the pastor or one's peers. They have a text book to go by in the case of trouble. On the other hand, the person who lives outside knows he doesn't know all the answers. Things will come up sooner or later that doesn't fit into a neat little package. Consequently when things don't go according to Hoyle, the person with all the answers needs to have redundancy, a back up system as to why his concept of God or his prayers didn't come in the vein expected. The one who does not have all the answers has no back up system; he still believes even though his doubts are intensified.

On one occasion, the Pharisees brought a woman known for her risqué life-style. They expected Jesus to throw stones at her, but he turned the tables on them. He said to the brave souls entrusted with their ready, rolled Scripture, ". . . He that is without sin among you, let him first cast a stone at her" (John 8:7 RSV). They all left; he had bested them with his insight.

Thus one will live in fear, anxiety, guilt or helplessness without his security blanket. The other still maintains his beliefs, although with the ability to alter them in his own fashion. They can then express anger, show grief, feel sad or feel bad; and they can feel gladness and joy in spite of circumstances because their idea of life has a deeper relationship than rules which hinder, and theories which become binding, when they don't work.

And guess what? God won't be any the more sadden because someone questioned the layout of the land.

I have decided to give you another gift. I present to you a mask with no peep holes. Put it on for an hour or two. Now use all of your other senses to see what is going on around you. For now just listen. I want you to hear the sounds around you. After awhile go outside. Visualize the path you will take. You know your backyard well enough to get to where you are going; if not start out in the middle of the yard. Pretend it is raining; feel the soft rain hit on you; and now hear it as it drops on the banana leaf nearby. A bird flutters by, and off in the distance you hear the sweet coo of a dove as she calls her mate to her side. How does this make you feel? Practice this until you can sense the other person with whom you love and all those with whom you know standing beside you. Learn to see with your 'ears' as Mary did when she knew she was to have a child.

To this end we need to grow when we have our eyes open. Now we can concentrate on our human condition with all our senses afire. If we can shift our attention span to our senses, can we not create a new mode of human existence? When the other person speaks, we hear the melody of his voice as well as see him or her differently. When we sit alone or when we are with another, we are in harmony with mother nature. More importantly, we stop caring if the other person is dark, fair, cute, obese or tanned. Try to become a whole body seer.

Next, we are going to use the same mask to create something. Many say they have no creativity. That is not true. You have a vast amount of knowledge stored in your brain which you can't recall. Hopefully you will learn to avail yourself of these charms. There are two things which you can visualize. First it may be very practical. You may have a project on which you are puzzled. It may be a design or an arrangement of some sort. Put on your mask. Now try to see what you are building. Here you must want desperately to see the object of your attention. Now take the dream you have to go backwards to see what it was before you finished the project. How are you going to take this object to trim it to your needs? Think about it in your soul, in the 'camp' with your eyes closed. This is your potential for imagery which you have had all along. Artists create from this kind of perception, why can't we?

Let's say you want to make a flower garden out of your back yard. You have looked at books; you have talked to others; somehow, though, you are perplexed. Now visualize what you want to see. How will you get there? Take the project one step at a time. Your inner self has already been working on this, so why not ask it. How, you ask? Ideas will pop into your head from nowhere. Write them down as you go. At night dreams will occur which you will have dismissed before, but now you need to put a pen and pencil by your bed, because if you don't write these things down, you may forget. Dreams do give us insight from some long past imagery which has been stored in our sub-conscious mind; so why not analyze them? Talk to someone about them to get their input.

This is helping us to use our right brain to create a spatial perception of the things we wish to do which before we just said, "I can't." You will be surprised at the solutions, plots, models, designs and characterizations you produce. Just remember, when Jesus sees the 5000, he asks for food to feed them; the disciples say it is too much to try to feed them. We cannot possibly feed them they argue. Jesus sees a way to complete the assignment (John 6:5-14).

The next possibility comes in terms of using our blindness to create a verbal description or pictorial vision of our beatific view. You probably think that you don't have a vivid imagination. Well we shall see. Please envision yourself in your backyard again, but this time you have planted a flower garden. Write down the words you see as we go along. Don't let me put words in your head. You are the thinker here. There are flowers in bloom, full grown; others are in the bud. From where did they come? How do they smell? Can you see them in your mind? Write down what you see, feel, smell and hear for there are sounds coming from those things around, like crickets chirping, birds singing, cars passing by and somewhere a radio may be playing. Write down every word that comes to your mind, in no particular order. Write what you feel, what you sense. No matter how inane, write it down.

In this view, add the one you love. How do they fit into your image? How do they compare to this grand view? Write it down. Use all those words you thought you had forgotten. After this experience is over, try to put those words into some sort of order. You will create a masterpiece of your own visualization when you do. Nobody else can do that. It won't matter if it doesn't rhyme. Some of the better thoughts never do anyway. Spend some time on it and you can make it rhyme if you wish. The idea is to put down your thoughts as you experienced them, what you felt, saw, heard, touched, smelled and could almost taste. And you thought you didn't have a vivid imagination!

Here's what I sensed:

A Flower in Bloom

A tiny seed planted in darkness does loom,
Until a flower in bud becomes a bloom,

A sacrifice of youth as God intended,
Adulthood with all its energy extended,
To a magnificent array of splendor,
With poignancy in color as its render.

E'en with all your charm, you are yesterday's child,
A flower in her deepest bloom of the wild,
Wiser now, yet of the past there is a trace,
An inner self which portrays youthful grace,
Matchless in poise even though a tinge of fall,
Courageous still for whatever might befall.

As time beats on and as the days take their toil,
My constant love for you they shall never foil,
For my flower will always have its sweet bloom;
So when earth takes back my seed to its drear tomb,
I will forever hold your aroma dear,
And await your full blossom in that fair year.

The one thing that seems to thwart our daily lives is stress. Stress comes from our activity triggered by natural causes or persons within our lives. Many of the stress related problems stem from our taking life too seriously. We rush hither and yon for no apparent reason than to get somewhere 15 minute to an hour early to do nothing. As I indicated earlier, slow down. I know you think the work you have to do at the office won't get done without you. If you can't make it because of sickness, it will get done or be there for you when you return. Take it seriously, but take it in stride. When you leave work, lock it up in the camp.

Somewhere along the way we must learn to become the person we are at the moment where we find ourselves. Switch gears from the office person to father, mother, friend, lover or sibling and vice versa. Then treat yourself to a little R&R. Take time to be alone to do your thing. Absorb yourself in a hobby, reading or a good movie. Plan to visit the pumpkin patch often. After you relax, you then can re-tackle those strenuous tasks which have held you captive for so long. There are a number of things you need to do to take charge of your life. The autonomous thinker will allow himself or herself to transcend the ordinary, routine problems which haunt our every day life. Here are a few suggestions.

    1.   Practice talking to someone who knows you well. Hopefully it will be your mate. Discuss the issues until the stress ebbs to the point you can move on with the day.

2.   Then engage in some exercise, something fun. It does not have to be physical training, but something to put your mind on rather than the day's problems.

2. Learn to lose. One of the things our society does is teach that the only thing in life is to win. Learn to not be so competitive. It is okay to compete, but do so where you can feel good about having played your very best. On this day someone was just better and you are proud of them. Besides, being successful is more important than success. You can be a winner and lose.

3. Think inspirational thoughts. You don't have to read devotions, but read life stories or watch them on television where the person becomes a hero by overcoming adversity. They never give up, but they didn't have it made either. Listen to your favorite kind of music. Hear the words they sing. They are closer to the truth than the platitudes you sometimes hear on Sunday.

4. Try to realize how much more work you can get done if you harness up your 'go' train to the energy you have pounding inside. Make the most of the inner struggles. Would you rather feel sorry for yourself or would you rather use the time to conquer some tangled webs in your soul?

5. You are not a robot. A robot can only do the things programmed inside, so why not realize you have limitations also. If you think the robot won't break down, think again. So will you. Know your capabilities and stay within the speed limit. We are taught not to procrastinate; well maybe we should re-look at this. There are some things that can absolutely wait until tomorrow. Learn to discern the necessary things. Then let the others go; you owe it to yourself.

6. Learn how to handle anger. Anger is a perfectly acceptable emotion if controlled. Jesus had anger and he expressed it when the situation called for it (1 Peter 2:23; Matt. 12:32; John 2:13-16). The right use of anger is by no means incompatible with love. There are some ways to control your anger. Look at the situation. If you are feeling good about yourself, you want get trapped in a no- win situation. Next what is your interpretation of the event? If your anger is focused on someone's destructive

pattern of behavior, then get angry at the deed and not the person. Try to be objective. If you have deep anger and it won't go away, find something, not someone, to cast it on. Be in charge of your life; don't let someone else push your buttons. Again you may want to harness anger to use the drive in doing something constructive you have been putting off. Here are some tips as to when anger becomes harmful:

a. When one is backed into a corner and his inner self strikes out because he feels he has to fight or flee. He becomes mad at his weakness and he gets angry to protect himself. The autonomous person knows this and works on the inner problem.

b When one feels resentment at the success of others. Resentment stops the flow of grace from one person to another.

c. When pain or harm is inflicted to gratify our wounded pride.

d. When our immaturity causes us to see red. This is like a child who throws a fit in the grocery because he wants a coke and his mother said no.

7. Look around you. You have been blessed more than most people. If so, count it all joy. Try to live a life of gratitude. Learn to be content.

I am reminded of the story Frankl told in his book, "Man's Search For Meaning".

It seems a servant claimed he had met death and he feared for his life. He begged the master to give him a horse so he could escape to Teheran. He received his horse to leave for the safe zone. The master then meets death and asked why he caused his servant harm. Death replied, "I didn't threaten him. I only showed surprise at finding him here when I was supposed to meet him tonight in Teheran" (pg 89).

Perhaps I should say a few words about resentment before we continue. Resentment occurs when:

1. You hold on to someone or something you do not like. You feel trapped. You feel guilty if you make a change.

2. You are suspicious of everyone's motives. Actually you wish you had thought of doing it first.

3.   You feel hopeless in ever changing the person or institute you love. Remember, it is you that you must change, not them.

4.   You are jealous.

5.   Consequently, you live with your fears; you feel alone and full of self-doubt. Therefore you hold on the usual ruts to which you are accustomed.

The autonomous person can allow himself to change. He will allow himself to change the circumstance if necessary. Remember life is a dance. You play the tune. God is not brother, father or the great grandfather who bestows life's blessing without struggle. He is the one who understands our cry of help in our constant confession, "I believe; help my unbelief." The more we take responsibility for ourselves, the more we will become one with him. We do not have to feel guilty for our actions if they release us from resentment, whether in a strained relationship or position. We can use creativity to serve Jesus in any capacity to which we decide. One thing for sure, he wants us to live authentically as friends, not slaves (John 15:15). The good news resounds: God still loves us no matter whether we were reacting to inner insecurities or if we were right. If the former, we can ultimately change those through maturity, or transcendence. Oh, and one more thing, if you make a decision, never, ever look back. You chose the road, now travel it. Later, if you have gone in the wrong direction, you have the freedom to blaze a new trail.

Conclusion

All of us wear several hats. In one given day we are husband, wife, employee, employer, parent, child, student and etc. In every role underneath we are still the person called. We assume the roles, but the roles should not consume us. Hopefully we have found ourselves in the process of becoming totally human, armed with compassion. Having compassion does not mean we are naïve to the point that we don't recognize evil must be stopped. When our children do those things that bring hardship on the family and themselves, they must be handled. When dictators like Saddam flaunt evil in the face of those who love freedom, he must be punished. When an employee causes friction and breaks the rules, he or she must be reprimanded. There are times anger must be stressed in positive ways to curb chaos.

No matter what your vocation, you can give yourself to it without fear you are not less loved because you don't do something else with your life. If you don't like your position, find another one. If not, learn to be content. What you are underneath is what counts. The autonomous person knows he is okay. Autonomous people do daily their assumed roles without really realizing they necessarily live a compassionate life. It is second nature to them. Others will try to get you to assume roles suited to them; however only do them if you have the time. Otherwise, say no. You don't have to feel guilty because you don't do the things someone expects because you live a life you choose; everywhere you go, you are the same; people know you care as you go.

In Henry Van Dyke's marvelous little book, (which by the way, it is a must read) "The Other Wise Man," Artaban, a Persian, has read the signs of the one who was to be born King in the days of Augustus Caesar when Herod ruled in Jerusalem. He sells all he had to take three jewels to the

Prince who is worthy to be served. The stones are a sapphire, a ruby and a pearl. He leaves to meet the three other Magi to go to worship the Prince.

On the journey, he meets a person who would surly die if he did not attend him. However, if he did he would miss his companions. He stays to care for the wounded person with much agony of soul for he really wanted to meet the coming One. He takes care of the venerable person all night until finally at dawn the sick one revives. Artaban strikes out; only the three Magi have gone when he does arrive at the juncture. They did leave a note for him to follow on behind.

In order to make the trip across the desert, he has to sell his sapphire to get the necessary supplies for the journey. He proceeds on his journey, coming to Bethlehem with a certain feeling of dread hanging in the air. He hears a woman's voice singing; he enters her abode to inquire of the baby Jesus. She tells him the Magi have come and gone. The parents have fled the area because Herod is killing all the new born baby boys in order to kill any usurper to his throne. Suddenly there arises a clamor outside; the woman becomes frighten because she has a baby boy within the range of Herod's decree. Artaban bribes the Captain of the guard with the second of his gifts to Jesus, the ruby, to save her son.

He then proceeds with his quest to find Jesus to give him his last gift. He travels for some 29 more years searching, to no avail. Finally he arrives in Jerusalem where again the uncertainty of the times fills him with an awareness something has happened to bring gloom all around. Worn and weary, he arrives there for one last look for the King. He joins a crowd to inquire as to the cause of the agitation in the air. They tell him of Jesus' death on the cross. He had thought to find him and now it is too late. If he could have gotten here earlier, perhaps he could have paid for his redemption with the last of the jewels, the pearl. As he stumbles along, his quest seemingly over, he meets a little Persian girl who has been taken as a slave to pay her father's debts. After a deep struggle within himself, he gives the pearl to the young girl to save her.

When he gave the pearl to the girl, the earth convulsed heavily. Stones came from everywhere, one hitting him on the temple. As he lay on the ground dying, the girl heard voices; she draws closer to hear: "Not so, my Lord: for when saw I thee an hungered and fed thee? Or thirsty, and gave thee drink? When saw I thee a stranger, and took thee in? Or naked, and clothed thee? When saw I thee sick or in prison, and came unto thee?" And then she heard a voice very faint and far away say, "Verily I say unto thee, Inasmuch as thou hast done it unto one of the least of these my brethren, thou has done it unto me."

We do it because it is who we are. You can't buy this at the market. You find it in your soul, awaken by a higher calling than yourself. Inasmuch as we have had our own wounds, hopefully to overcome them, we can understand the wound in others. Through our calling we become one in their pain. Only until we see a great light to lead us out of our darkness will we reach our ultimate destination.

Sitting on Momma's Porch

The wind, flowing through the trees,
A caressing, gentle breeze,
Reminds me of long ago,
Rocking easy, to and fro,
Sitting on Momma's porch.

Oh, we laughed throughout the day,
And whiled the long hours away;
Yes, carefree as we did roam;
How I long to be at home,
Sitting on Momma's porch.

There was built a lot of hope,
Each had eyes which telescope,
To scan all the distant stars,
And e'en plan to visit Mars,
Sitting on Momma's porch.

I know I can live that dream,
Live peacefully and serene,
As those moments were back then,
All those golden minutes when,
Sitting on Momma's porch.

About the Author

This is the author's first book other than a Doctor of Ministry project submitted to New Orleans Baptist Theological Seminary in 1977 to complete his Doctorate degree. He has also written several poems which are in print on the Poetry.com web sight.

In addition, he wrote, in the seventies, a weekly column for a weekly newspaper.

The author served as pastor for 18 years in various churches and now serves as relief Chaplain for a Catholic Hospital in Alexandria, LA. (St. Francis Christos Cabrini).